D0184465

God and Ourselves

NORMAN W. COX

God
and
Ourselves

BROADMAN PRESS
Nashville, Tennessee

Library of Congress catalog card number 60-5191
Printed in the United States of America
5. JE59KSP.

To O. M. C. and our children, G. W. C. and S. C. T.

Preface

IN JULY, 1909, I made my first effort to preach a sermon from a text in the fifteenth chapter of Luke. Since that time I have found forty-four other sermons in that passage, forty-one of them from the prodigal son section. About eight years ago the idea possessed me that in these thirty-two verses Luke has given us a condensed summary of the Bible's full revelation of God and ourselves. What he has presented there has been repeated in varying degree in the experience of every man to whom the revelation of God has been given. What follows is one preacher's understanding of this marvelous message.

My gratitude needs to be expressed to Dr. J. W. Storer and to Dr. Lynn E. May, Jr., for reading the manuscript and making helpful corrections; to Judson B. Allen for valuable editorial help in revising, reorganizing, supplementing, and styling the manuscript; and to Mrs. Richmond O. Brown for the secretarial production of it.

Contents

ix

1

God and Ourselves

> *Now the tax collectors and sinners*
> *were all drawing near to hear him.*
> *And the Pharisees and the scribes*
> *murmured, saying, "This man re-*
> *ceives sinners and eats with them."*
> *So he told them this parable.*
>
> LUKE 15:1–3, RSV

ON AN OCTOBER SUNDAY AFTERNOON in 1928 while I was listening to a radio sermon by Harry Emerson Fosdick, I heard him say: "Every man's life is an island lifted up out of the sea of life, around which Jesus rows until he comes to the point of greatest need. There he lands and tarries until he has met that need or that soul has finally scorned him."

That statement caught me. It stopped me from listening further to what he had to say, and in my mind I traveled through the Gospels to see if it were true. Within a few days I had read them carefully again. Since that time I have remembered the statement. Its relevance has been fully confirmed. It is a fact that every time Jesus has come into contact with a person or group in the days of his flesh—or since, ei-

1

ther through his gospel or by his Holy Spirit—he has landed at the point of greatest need. It was so with Simon who became Peter, Nathaniel, the woman at the well, and all the others. When the greatest need is met, the solution of the smaller ones follows. Once the new birth occurs, one becomes a new creature in Christ. Then he is a true son of God, with a far greater dignity and destiny than ever before remotely could have been his. In the gospel every soul is confronted with the opportunity to become the best that the compassionate grace of God offers. This gift of grace meets the greatest need in the life of every man.

One picture is worth a thousand words; one vivid instant from life is worth full volumes of generalization. In the parable of the father and his two sons Jesus painted a picture of God and ourselves. In it he summarized what the Bible has to say on that subject. When God wanted to tell the world for all time the message of redeeming love, he did not write a book of theology. He sent a Person, his only begotten Son. The life, teachings, death, and resurrection of Jesus Christ is the gospel. His continuing presence in the Holy Spirit is its confirmation.

Thus also did Jesus himself. He did not make theological pronouncements. He spoke in parables. He told realistic stories about realistic people. Ultimately he could not really explain himself in any other way.

Have we not erred in shortening this greatest of all parables, the one of the father and his two sons, by having in our thinking included in it only the younger son although, as a matter of fact, when Jesus spoke it he specifically declared, "There was a man who had two sons"? The elder brother is as much a part of the parable as is his junior brother. In all of it our Saviour is telling us of the contrasting ways by which sin ensnares all kinds of men.

This larger parable of the two sons is a picture of God and ourselves, of God dealing with all mankind. In it are implied all the truths of the gospel, distilled into the essence of a single drama. In it we have God and man, sin and salvation, the motives of prayer, the freedom of man's choice, the cause of his disobedience, inescapable judgment, the fruits of folly, the insidious delusions of self-righteousness, the critical crises of decision, the recognition of guilt, contrite confession in contrast with self-justifying hypocritical pretensions, the boundless riches of the divine mercy, and the marvelous manifestation of the fact that "when God forgives, he gives."

Throughout the longer parable God is a loving Father. We and all the multitudes who share in our humanity have been divided in it into two groups—the sons who are publicans and sinners and those who are scribes and Pharisees. Face to face with Jesus for the first time, every man is a publican or a Pharisee, and each is a sinner needing a Saviour. The two are radically opposite in their attitudes. Their characters and their places in this profound, inclusive story can lead us to genuine self-understanding. They are the point of beginning —they, and their reaction to Jesus. Within or between them lies the context that determines the response of men when they first meet the Son of God.

The Publicans and Sinners

Those called publicans and sinners in Jesus' day were not pagans who worshiped idols or devotees of some strange religious cults. The publicans were quislings. They collaborated with the Roman authorities to collect taxes on the basis of financial profit to themselves. This made them religious outcasts from their own people. They had sold life's most important loyalty for financial reward.

The ones called sinners were religious untouchables, also

ostracized from their Jewish faith. Either unashamed immorality, dishonesty, or unbelief had separated them from the faith of their fathers.

Publicans and sinners had one thing in common: They had, at least in some measure, weighed their ancestral religion in the balances and, as far as they were concerned, had found it wanting. They had rejected it, and nothing was left. Painfully they had learned that neither material wealth nor sensual gratification could feed the innate hunger of their souls. Experience had brought them only boredom in license, only fatigue in sensuality. Their hearts were heavy with the misery which follows alienation from God. Hope had fled their hearts. For them life had become a journey into hopelessness.

Then One Day They Met Jesus

Immediately they were fascinated by what they saw and heard. They sensed his compassion and were bewildered. Here was a religious Teacher who pointed no scornful finger at their sins, though indeed he knew them all. He did not seem offended. He did not reject them, nor did he pass by them on the other side of the street to escape the defilement of their company. Instead, he was their occasional guest, their friend. He talked with them, accepted their hospitality. He never berated them. Yet what he said, verily what he was, made them despise themselves. He possessed none of the things for which they had deserted their race and sold their souls. He wanted none of these things, for he knew also what they had found in their purchasing—the bitterness of frustrated hunger of soul. Suddenly they wanted what he had—peace with God. Wrapped in the power of his compassionate personality, they longed for a new way, a new life, a new truth.

In Jesus they found an open door to hope. From the early days of his public ministry and until the cross, they sought him in increasing numbers. For him they forsook the vanities of sensualism and materialism which had deceived them and took hold of the sure promises of God. They found happy peace in Jesus Christ.

The Scribes and Pharisees

In the days of Jesus the scribes and Pharisees were two closely allied but distinct groups. Together they were the most influential civic, social, and religious leaders of the Jewish people.

The scribes were religious professionals. It might be fair to call them Jewish Jesuits. They were an ancient order of the interpreters of the Mosaic code and of the Levitical statutes. Throughout many generations they had built up voluminous commentaries, glossing in great detail every minute point of the Jewish moral and ceremonial law. Eventually their commentaries became religious traditions with more authority than the inspired Scriptures which they interpreted. This substitution of their own tradition for the Word of God brought them pointed condemnation from Jesus and sowed the seeds of their bitter hatred for him.

These scribes had vested interests throughout the Jewish world. They were teachers in the synagogues. They served as judges over their own interpretations, applying their traditions to the problems of everyday life. Their influence grew; their authority was more and more respected. The honor accorded them was great.

The Pharisees were much more numerous than the scribes. They were a special religious fraternity. They were close to the people. Their vows of membership to their order had committed them to hazard all for their faith. In previous

The Self-righteous and the Unrighteous Meet
Each Other

Only the most radical and unusual circumstances could
have brought these two groups into immediate contact with
each other in the same crowd. The heart of each was filled
with bitter contempt toward the other. Is it not interesting
that Jesus was the focal point of their contact? They came to
hear him from opposite motives. There is the mystical draw-
ing power of God of which Jesus spoke when he said, "And I,
when I am lifted up from the earth, will draw all men to myself" (John 12:32, RSV) . Sooner or later Jesus stands at the
heart's door of every man to whom the word of his gospel has
been given. He is the inescapable Christ. To him the bur-
dened sinner goes with a contrite heart, longing for pardon
and peace. The critical Pharisee is mysteriously moved by the
amazing magnetism of Jesus to confront him with his scorn.
Although he will not believe, he has felt the power of Jesus'
message and personality.

One who has been trained in psychology sees in these critics
of Jesus and their successors through the centuries a continuing group that is persistently determined to crucify Christ.
Their violent reaction against him declares the fact that they
are mortally afraid of him. His insight into the ghastly iniquity of their deluded and disturbed hearts fills them with
panic. In their terror they became desperate. Their pride in
their own opinion and position leads most of them to prefer
to go to hell rather than change their minds and attitudes.

Surely this explains the motivation that brought the
mixed crowd together in the presence of Jesus. One group
gathered to hear him, and his love and understanding broke
their hearts. They were led to abhor their sins. They believed
in him, and he became their Saviour.

But his critics condemned him: "This man receives sinners and eats with them." It was the worst thing they thought they could say about him. Their minds, blinded in their self-seeking righteousness from an understanding of the Spirit of truth, uttered this judgment in condemnation because they had believed a lie rather than God. So many still are as they were.

In response to this approach of these opposite groups Jesus answered with three immortal spiritual pictures—three simple stories: the parable of the lost sheep; the parable of the lost coin; and the parable of the lost sons.

Each of these is a part of the story of God's grief over sinners and his act of concern for their redemption. Together they produce a powerful witness. They summarize all that the Bible has to declare about the central meaning of the attitude of God and sinners toward him and each other.

The first two parables are introductory. Sheep and coins are not so important as sons. They do shed light on the climactic parable. They prepare us for the supreme metaphor of our Bible, the supreme truth of our faith—the Father God whose worshipers are his children, children by creation, children by redemption, children by adoption. This is God's answer to criticism. This is the Saviour's response to the need of publicans and sinners. In this story is the gospel—in summary, the full revelation of God and ourselves for every person in the world.

2

Man's First Prayer

"Father, give me . . ."
LUKE 15:12, RSV

SOONER OR LATER all men pray.

The small city's boldest atheist had been ill for months. His end was near. He lived alone in his large ancestral home. There were no near relatives to be grieved by his going. He was so alone that there seemed to be no one who hoped to inherit his substantial estate. The doctor, a hired housekeeper, and a trained nurse were practically the only ones who saw him in his last days.

Yet there was a younger man who cared. A few years before, they had been friends. They had similar ideas. Then the younger one came to know Christ. Thereafter he was away from home much of the time, bearing witness to his new faith. He had prayed much for his older friend. The sufferer had repelled every effort he made. But each time at the end of the visit the lonely sinner begged his younger friend to come to see him whenever he could.

The atheist's death was not far away. His Christian friend decided to see him again and make a full-length try to break down the doors of his resistance. Immediately upon his arrival he said: "You know I once thought as you do. Then I became acquainted with Jesus Christ. I saw how totally mistaken I had been. I heard the invitation of Jesus, believed him, accepted him. He became my Lord and Saviour. He can and will save you if you will call upon him in believing, surrendering faith. Won't you let me pray with you?"

The man so near to death interrupted: "I have lived an atheist, I will die one."

When the distressed friend left, the nurse followed him outside. She said: "Do not let him fool you. I was outside the door and heard what occurred. I have nursed him for months. Many times when he did not think I was near enough to hear, I have heard him pray. His stubborn pride and the habit of the years enslave him. He seems to have chosen to try to beg God in secret to save him in spite of his atheism."

There are few men, if any, who never pray. Jesus knew this, and he put into the mouth of the prodigal two petitions which epitomize all prayer.

Every prayer that man has ever prayed has sprung from one of two opposite motives. They are as far apart as east and west.

They are:

"Father, give me!"

"Father, make me!"

Sometimes there is a mixture of both.

The first is the prayer of a self-willed spirit. It is the natural prayer of a soul that desires escape from the authority of God. It wants what it wants without any limitations. Its final end is want.

The second is the prayer of submission. At first such a prayer is never easy. Few, if any, ever pray it with sincerity until tragic failure and utter despair drive them to it. Its results are always satisfying.

The Point of Sin's Beginning

Self-will is the primary point of sin's beginning in all known experience. In the Garden of Eden Satan confronted man with the challenge of God's integrity and an offer of divine equality. A review of the story of that fateful meeting shows the devil beginning it by asking Eve an impertinent question: "Did God say, 'You shall not eat of any tree of the garden'?"

She replied: "We may eat of the fruit of the trees of the garden; but God said, 'You shall not eat of the fruit of the tree which is in the midst of the garden, neither shall you touch it, lest you die.' "

Satan countered: " 'You will not die. For God knows that when you eat of it your eyes will be opened, and you will be like God, knowing good and evil.' So when the woman saw that the tree was good for food, and that it was a delight to the eyes, and that the tree was to be desired to make one wise, she took of its fruit and ate; and she also gave some to her husband, and he ate" (Gen. 3:1–6, RSV).

Here Satan assumed the role he has always played in dealing with people. He offered himself as the world's first professor of religious education. From that beginning he has never deviated either in his pedagogy or the substance of his curriculum.

He commenced his lecture with a question which implied that God had arbitrarily denied Eve and her husband the right to eat of the delectable fruit of all the trees in the garden.

Eve promptly corrected the false implication. They could eat of all of them except one. Out of love for them God had warned them not to eat of it because its fruit contained a fatal poison.

The professor was probably silent for a moment before he startled her with his assertion: "You will not die. God has not told you the truth. He has selfishly prohibited you from the best fruit of the garden. He is jealous of his superiority over you, because he knows that if you eat of that tree you and your husband will no longer be inferior to him. Would you not like to be equal with God?"

Before that, neither Adam nor Eve had had the slightest doubt of their Creator's honesty. The leaven of this new doubt soon penetrated their thinking. They had been completely happy. No ungratified desire had disturbed their satisfaction. Their hearts had been filled with a rewarding sense of the goodness of God. So perfect was their life and relationship that they had not in the least been aware of either inferiority or dissatisfaction.

But Satan was so plausible. Eve soon began to wonder, in spite of herself. Perhaps she had been naïve. Could it be that this handsome, sophisticated stranger was right? His promises were so attractively and persuasively presented. Here was a daring thought that offered a thrilling prospect.

How long it took the lies of the devil to capture the minds of Adam and Eve so that they were willing to gamble all they had for the vision of equality with God no one can ever know. The experience of all men sooner or later confirms that these verses from Genesis describe sin's tragic entrance into human experience. In essence sin has always been the fruit of the perverted ambition which seeks to possess the promises of the delusion that one may himself possess the stature of God in his own small universe.

The Measure of Our Spiritual Inheritance

The full measure of human depravity cannot be fully understood unless one realizes the scope and quality of man's original spiritual inheritance. The description of creation has a simple face but contains unplumbed depths of meaning. Far more is comprehended than has generally been recognized in the Genesis statements: "Then God said, 'Let us make man in our image, after our likeness; and let them have dominion. . . .' So God created man in his own image, in the image of God he created him. . . . And God blessed them" (Gen. 1:26–28, RSV) .

The key to the meaning of the creation of man is the phrase "the image of God." By it we can know that God creatively communicated or transferred from himself into the nature and being of man certain godlike qualities, elements of being or personality that only he possesses and that no other genus or order of beings in the universe has ever possessed.

What are they? At least six of these distinctively divine elements are evident in man's life.

The first is imagination. This is the power by which the musician hears the melody before it is composed, the artist sees the picture before it is painted, the engineer rears the bridge before it is built or the architect the cathedral before it is erected. That quality enabled God to see the universe and man and all that is in them before they came to be. Beyond question, man possesses this godlike attribute. It is the womb out of which all of this world's great progress has been born.

The second divine element is reason—the power to think, to form and fashion judgments, to develop hypotheses, to experiment, to discover, to extend the bounds of what is to the realization of what can be. These are qualities which God has in himself which he has shared with men.

The third is the power to produce the first act, to do something that has not been done before, to make a beginning when the end is not in sight, and to persevere through obstacles until an end is reached.

The fourth is freedom of choice. Man is free. He is faced with alternatives, and he is bound by the choices he makes.

The fifth is moral discernment. Man not only chooses, but he also places a value on his choices. He can tell good from evil. He can evaluate, by his prevision, in advance the effects of the choices he makes. In the exercise of this element he derives from his choices a sense of guilt or innocence, remorse or spiritual peace.

The sixth is memory. In one special aspect this trait is unique in man and God. It sustains the consciousness of life's continuity while it holds in man's unconscious mind the meaning of all that he has learned. It is man's wisdom; it is his guide in the choices of daily living. When into man's memory is poured history, the experience of men with each other, and revelation, the experience of men with God, man has received the image of God's immortality. By means of memory a man stores up his own personal experience with God and thereby increases his awareness of God. When he accepts Christ to be Lord and Saviour, he acquires the dimension of the new birth. Thereafter, his memory acquires vast treasures but continually increases his apperception of his spiritual resources.

In all these ways we were made to be like God; we were given his image. God shared with us as much of his nature as it was possible for him to share. We have received from him a dignity, a potential, and a responsibility that should constantly amaze and challenge us. This is why sin is so blasphemously evil: by an act of sin man repudiates and loses all of this genuine godlikeness. His vain and futile ambition to be more godlike makes him only less so and leaves him with only the depraved husks of his former image.

The Propulsive Power of Sin

The man-made, earth-circling satellites furnish a helpful illustration for understanding the propulsive power of sin. Why do these satellites keep circling the earth for so long after they are separated from the original thrust that propelled them into space and removed them from the earth's surface? Those who know tell us that they were hurled beyond the earth's atmosphere, which would have acted as a brake to retard their speed, at an attained velocity and direction which enables them to continue circling the earth in practically the same orbit in which they first began to move around it. The pull of gravity created by the earth's mass holds them on their course with only slight loss of distance or speed.

The destroying spiritual force of disobedience (unbelief in the integrity and truth of the word of God) in the act of the first man and woman created a counter spiritual thrust that hurled them out of the orbit of their relationship to God into the orbit of Satan's dominance. Succeeding generations of unregenerated human beings, bound in the depravity of a fixation of disbelief and disobedience, have continued to circle in Satan's orbit because the power of self-will propelled them to desire to live their lives independently of God. The basic primary delusions that sin creates in the sinner are that God is not to be trusted; that he, the sinner, is capable of successfully managing his own life; and therefore he must get what he wants and use it as he chooses. Acting upon these delusions results in the age-old spiritual rat-race wherein the soul of an unbelieving man chases to his doom the illusion that he can become a god by despising his Creator and worshiping himself. Out of this illusion all tragedy has been derived. It is as deadly today as it ever has been at any time. It is the final spiritual life story of all who are never born again of God.

Jesus knew this. He had seen and known it all from the beginning. It was to redeem man from this sin that he had been born into this world. We should not be surprised, then, that on that day when the publicans and sinners gathered to hear him and the Pharisees and scribes murmured, as he began to tell them and us about *God* and *ourselves* in the parable, he said the younger son prayed, "Father, give me."

His Father God had heard that prayer a thousand times and more from every person who had ever lived. He had seen every man take the gifts of God and squander them as that prodigal did. We need to remember that the story Jesus told is the final spiritual biography of every man—but for the redeeming grace of God. Therefore, each of us is the younger son, and we have prayed as he prayed, "Father, give me."

Here we should recall that Jesus is looking for the place of our greatest need that he may land and meet it. Here it is. He is eager to find us. We are evasive. We do not see ourselves as he sees us. Our thoughts are not his thoughts, nor are our ways his ways. We keep on praying, "Father, give me." Father, give me what?

The Detailed Specifications

We mention many things, but the determining motivation is the same—let me have what I want when I want it without any restrictions regarding its use.

The prodigal did not pray to be given his father's integrity, wisdom, faith, or reverence. He despised the qualities of his father's high character. He instinctively loathed the virtues which condemned him by comparison at every turn. He wanted escape from his father, thinking that thereby he would escape his own innate inferiority.

Like men of today, he coveted material things. He begged for goods, worldly possessions with a high dollar value. His appetite craved sensual enjoyments beyond the level of wholesome normality. He was interested in passion, obsession, even perversion. He prayed to his father for the gift of money, which he thought could purchase prestige to exalt his self-esteem. He wanted a fortune to spend in adorning his idolatrously inflated dreams of his own importance.

Even more, he wanted freedom. His prayer, "Give me," was a plea for release from his obligation to his father. He wanted to escape the responsibility of being his father's son. In the far country he could stand on his own feet and make his own position. He was certain that the change would improve his situation. He was like a rebellious adolescent, and he covered up his feeling of inferiority by pretending to be superior.

Souls in revolt against God want no part of him. They must worship something less than God, so they worship themselves. They make themselves a religion of their own. They change the truth of God into a lie and worship and serve the creature more than the Creator (Rom. 1:25, RSV). Such self-worshipers thus try to transform God into their image, rather than have him transform them into his image. Wherever men quit the God of the Bible, very soon they deify themselves or others.

But when men create their own gods, they create depraved gods. Men project and adorn their own worst qualities. Men apart from God are fascinated with their exalted conceit. This is because the most powerful thing in an unregenerated heart is depravity. Until a man is born again, he can never develop the thinking of spiritual maturity.

So it is that the godless pray. Some of the most godless persons say prayers regularly. Others who seem to forget God completely pray ardently in times of great danger. From both world wars came the oft-quoted saying, "There are no atheists in foxholes." Men spontaneously rush to God for deliverance when sudden death seems inescapable. Too many seem to want to be saved in their sin, not from it. Their prayer is for God to give them escape from the consequences of their wrong choices without requiring them to abhor the evil they have chosen.

The natural disposition of every man until he has confronted Jesus Christ is to justify himself. He wants God to humor his desires. He demands privileges he does not merit. In this first prayer the younger son spelled it out: "Father, give me the portion of goods that falleth to me." This was the presumptive and pre-emptory thinking of a foolish adolescent. This was the mind of an unbeliever—slanted and distorted by conceited illusions, mistaking foolish notions for smart thinking.

In this parable Jesus is holding before us the mirror of divine truth. He tells us deliberately that what this young man did, we have done. This parable is the true-to-life picture of ourselves. The young man was too much in love with himself to see the sin that Jesus saw in him. So it continued to be until a day months or years later when he discovered himself—friendless, forsaken, ragged, starving, and far from home.

The habit of praying, "Father, give me," strongly persists, even in Christians. Long after they come face to face with this picture of themselves and return from the far country away from God, they still pray it.

They are certainly Christians. With contrite hearts they made the long trek to the cross, confessed their sin, pled for mercy, and received God's gracious pardon. Then they prayed the second prayer of the parable, "Father, make me."

They were born again. They received Christ as Saviour and had life's most wonderful experience, the experience of becoming the spiritual sons of the living God. Then for a time —there followed an interval; it may have been days, weeks, months, or years—they had fellowship in Christ. But eventually they found themselves becoming involved in puzzling experiences. A strange coldness had chilled their glow. Their zest had evaporated. Their Christian experience had lost its luster. They continued to pray, but nothing happened. Sooner or later they came to a time of real crisis. In their desperation they finally discovered that the old habit of praying, "Father, give me," has a long hang-over.

It spoils much of the life of too many Christians. Self has regained the throne in their souls. They want God to give them what they want when they want it and as they want it. Ministers meet spiritual beggars like this distressingly often.

When I became her pastor, she was always present at every service. She had a husband, but it was months before I met him. It was generally known that he was a prosperous professional gambler. I tried to talk to her about making some effort to win him to Christ, but she was indifferent to my interest. One morning, some two years later, she breathlessly rushed into my study and abruptly exclaimed, "I want you to convert my husband, and I want you to do it in a hurry."

I answered, "For two years I have been trying to get you interested in your husband's salvation. You have been anything but co-operative. Why has it suddenly become so urgent this morning that he become a Christian?"

"You know that he has been a successful gambler for a long time," she said. "Recently he went into partnership with some men who are smarter operators than he is. They are gradually cleaning him out. He foolishly thinks he can still turn the tables on them and win. Nothing short of his getting religion will stop him. If that doesn't happen soon, he will be dead broke."

She wanted God to bail her out.

Wives, mothers, and fathers who previously had no concern suddenly become excited about the conversion of a member of the family when he shows signs of becoming an alcoholic. Actually, all they are asking God to do is to save them from the anxiety, embarrassment, expense, and annoyance of his indulgence. They really aren't interested in his soul, or even in him. They are thinking of themselves.

The mother of such a son besieged me for help. She gave me no rest from her importunity. I did my best to help him. She had another son who was as godless a sinner as could be found in that city. She never mentioned his need nor invited my help for him. One day I called her attention to that fact. Her answer was, "Why should I? He does not drink."

During the dreadful depression days we prayed earnestly for deliverance from its rigors. We wanted jobs that paid living wages and businesses that could be operated at a profit. We wanted to be more secure, enjoy luxuries, buy new cars, and take long vacations. Then Hitler set the world on fire, and the Japanese bombed Pearl Harbor. Suddenly everybody had jobs and money ran almost like water in the streets after a long, hard rain. But it was blood money. We could not spend it for cars; none were being made. We could not get gasoline or tires for the old cars we had. In 1944 the American people did not give into the Lord's treasury through his churches proportionately as much as they had in 1934.

This hang-over affects churches, Christian institutions, society at large, and even ministers, of whom better should be expected. It corrupts motives. It arms conceits and self-seeking. The spirit of Satan induces us to rationalize. Too many of us gild our vanity with some pious language and promote some holy proposals because we think that the good Lord will have to help us out to protect his own good name or to profit his own cause.

Some devout men and their wives have solemnly promised the Lord that if he would enable them to get an oil well on their land, they would give him a tithe of all the income from it, although they had not bothered to tithe their previous receipts. Or if it wasn't an oil well, it was some other speculative venture. The good Lord has never been impressed by such specious propositions. He is never interested in rushing a supply of fast money into the pockets of such "Father, give me," pleaders.

How perilous for the God-called minister is the temptation to slip into praying "Father, give me" prayers! I know. I have been a minister for fifty years and have had my share of such desires. The rationalizing technique overcomes us in a pattern similar to this: "Dear Lord, give us a church where every member loves all the other members. Grant us a membership that tithes so that there will be no financial handicaps to the work and thy cause will prosper. Create in the hearts of throngs of people a desire to attend the services that thy house may overflow. Yes, Lord, may the Holy Spirit convict and convert sinners every week so that we will need to baptize every Sunday."

These are good petitions. Many ministers have pressed on in arduously zealous effort to try to do their part to bring about God's answer. Some have grown discouraged and wondered why they were not more largely answered. Could it have been that, while they never said it to anyone and did not even hint it to God, yet deep within themselves there was the unspoken yearning for the enhancement of their reputations and the opening of doors to a more opulent opportunity that would follow the answer to such a prayer?

The most difficult temptation for even the best Christian to discern and overcome is to discover when and how Satan may have poisoned the springs from whence the motive to pray comes.

3

The Answer

And he divided his living between them.

LUKE 15:12, RSV

IN THE FATHER'S ANSWER to the prayer of the younger son, Jesus declares a fact about God that few have clearly perceived. We are either the younger son or his elder brother. His prayer is our universal prayer, the center of every selfish heart. Only after a transforming crisis is man delivered from it and given a new prayer: "Father, make me."

But all have sinned, all are selfish, and all share in the first prayer. Thus all share also in the answer: "And he divided his living between them." By this answer Jesus meant that God has actually given himself to each man, to all men, in a measure beyond anything they have remotely understood.

The primary purpose of Jesus' coming into the world was to redeem men and women from the curse of sin and death that they might in him be reborn the sons and daughters of the living God. In order to accomplish this purpose, he needed to bring to self-willed sinners a clear revelation of the nature, character, and purpose of his Father, God. Jesus described this mission when he said:

I thank thee, Father, Lord of heaven and earth, that thou hast hidden these things from the wise and understanding and revealed them to babes; yea, Father, for such was thy gracious will. All things have been delivered to me by my Father; and no one knows the Son except the Father, and no one knows the Father except the Son and any one to whom the Son chooses to reveal him. Come to me, all who labor and are heavy laden, and I will give you rest. Take my yoke upon you, and learn from me; for I am gentle and lowly in heart, and you will find rest for your souls (Matt. 11:25–29, RSV).

These words of Jesus are a commentary that begins to define what he meant when he said that the father "divided his living." The younger son and his elder brother, representing publicans and sinners and scribes and Pharisees, epitomize all the attitudes of all the people in the world toward God until they have seen him in Christ. Only Jesus is competent to interpret what he meant by "divided his living between them." In the presence of Jesus, we are face to face with the fact of the greatness and graciousness of God.

Man, created in the image of God, shared in the life and being of God. When he broke away from God by his sinful rebellion, he forfeited his original relationship with his Creator but did not destroy God's love for him. God continued to endow every newly begotten child with the image of God. To each child and all the children that have been born God has "divided his living between them." He has done this in the full awareness that they would despise their inheritance as Adam and Eve did. The greatness and graciousness of God in this eternal persistence amazes us. No matter how sinful we are, he continues to love us, to persist in giving himself to us, to defend us from dangers fatal to life, to provide for us beyond anything we recognize, and to call us with the voice of his Son. By the cords of his mercy he draws us, by the wooing of his grace he invites us, and by the yearning of his compassion he longs for partnership with us. He has put so much of himself into us that we are very dear to him. Even though man is forever trying to exploit God's goodness to gratify his own lusts and ambitions, God keeps on blessing him. The spiritual insanity that sin begets in these sons of men is manifest in their continued exaggeration of their self-importance. Their depravity produces in them a small opinion of God.

The greatness and graciousness of God is evident in the fact that he continues to love us, even though he is totally holy and his infinite knowledge enables him always to know all our evil desires and designs. The psalmist was aware of this:

> O Lord, thou hast searched me and known me!
> Thou knowest when I sit down and when I rise up;
>   thou discernest my thoughts from afar.
> Thou searchest out my path and my lying down,
>   and art acquainted with all my ways.
>   PSALM 139:1–3, RSV

Despite God's knowledge and his pursuing love, all the prodigals and their elder brothers of all the centuries have tried to run away from him and escape the sense of his presence. The answer of the father to the prayer of the prodigal is an enigma.

Why did he answer as he did?

He knew what this son would do with what he received. He knew what the results would be. He did not want the son to break away and abandon himself to a dissolute life. Why, then, did he not restrain the boy? Thinking as men think, there is no satisfactory answer. Could we think as God does, we would find the Father's full justification for the choice he made.

There are some truths about God's nature that illuminate the mystery of his action. God has limited his freedom by giving us ours. He has always permitted wilful human beings to have their way, whether that way be good or ill. This is natural and necessary. God created us in his image. A significant part of that image is the right of self-determination. This right God has given us, and he continues to respect it. He will not cancel his gift.

Some have thought that God made a mistake when he permitted men to pry into the secrets of atomic nature and to invent the hydrogen and cobalt bombs. But God has always acted thus. Discoveries of new power do indeed add to man's potential for sin and tragedy. Yet even more, they add to his potential for triumph. If he used these powers as the partner of God, they could become an incalculable benediction. God supremely yearns for men to desire his will and way, but he will not coerce them. Obedience to his law and gospel are not compulsory. He will never violate the sovereignty of man's right of choice. He perpetually entreats. He never forces. By the persuasion of love he strives with the spirit of man. He pleads for a real partnership with man. But the door is never locked against man's leaving. In plain language, man can go to hell, if that is his choice. If he does, it is because he has so determined.

God would rather have one soul to trust, love, and obey him from choice than the devotion of a million puppets who would be incapable of yielding to temptation. All the prodigals do not die in the "far country." The right to choose and the capacity to sin, repent, return to the forsaken Father with confession from a contrite heart, decide to serve him forever, and receive his kiss of pardon—these are considerations and compensations that manifest the wisdom of God's answer to man's first prayer.

While the son left the father, the father did not leave the son. The son tried to suppress his knowledge and memory of his father. He used his desires, dreams, and dissipations to the limit in an effort to escape the father. So it has ever been with those who have seen the light and tried to escape into darkness.

Both God and human parents face the fateful hour when children will be denied their rights if they are kept at home against their wills. Who can say it is not better for these young people to accept the responsibility they should not avoid? Can they develop courage, self-reliance, initiative, faith, and achievement without adventure? Wise fathers and mothers finally prove their faith in their sons and daughters by unleashing them to full liberty, but they are not indifferent. Neither is God. The children must leave home to go to college or to serve their country or to take a job far away. Their parents yearn for their return. Although separated by physical distances, parents are bound to their children through prayer and persuasive remembrance. So it is with God and us. No wonder so many "go back to father and home." God has planted something in the heart of all that calls them to "arise and go." Many do.

Surely it would not be irreverent or presumptuous to say that God's answers to our "Father, give me" prayers are a calculated risk he has assumed for each one of us.

Sin is a chain reaction and a downhill roll. At its very first assertion, human self-will is strong enough to break the bond between a man and his God. With exercise it becomes stronger and stronger, insulating the sinner more and more from any contact with the divine Source of his life. Soon the sinner comes to a place where God's blessings cannot be found. God cannot follow a sinner so far as to share in his iniquity. Man can go wherever he chooses, but when he subverts his spiritual inheritance to evil uses, God's holiness will not allow him to be a companion in the debauchery.

When man no longer feels the presence of God, his ego expands. He is deluded by the notion that he can provide for himself. He does not want God; he has no use for God. He stands in the center of his soap-bubble self-sufficiency, and his insulated soul withers and shrinks. The springs of his vitality dry up, and his world closes in upon him as the range of his vision contracts. He is dying, slowly and imperceptibly, but inexorably. He is a drying twig.

But there is hope of return. All men do not die. Some believe in proper prayer. Some are not cut off from God. Some live forever upon the vitality of his presence.

Who are these people? They are the children—the young in body and the young in Christ—and the old ones. They are the people at the two ends of life, those who are amazed in its thrilling newness and those who are looking forward to a new life with Christ.

Children whose minds are filled with wonder and whose souls have not been hardened by long experience of sin's perversion are responsive to God. They see and know the angels God sends to guard and guide them. They can feel God's presence in parents, friends, and churches. Beyond these the Spirit of the living God communicates with their yet unspoiled spirits. Their heavenly Creator will not suffer them to become unprotected spiritual orphans, adrift in a devil-dominated world. They must have special protection. Did not Jesus in speaking of them say, "For I tell you that in heaven their angels always behold the face of my Father who is in heaven" (Matt. 18:10, RSV)?

God has provided far more for them than we know. They pray. He answers. They know it. Have not most of us memories of our childhood that affirm this?

So it is with Christian youth. Youth is that thrilling section of life whose poems are not yet written, pictures yet unpainted, songs not yet sung, and dramatic adventures yet wait the fulfilment of the dream. In youth, imagination paints in living reality pictures of future greatness not yet achieved. Young people have not lost the sense of wonder. They can feel God's presence. Most of them pray. He answers. There is a sense of real communication.

Yet most of them in some fashion are in revolt against the world of adults, in rebellion against whatever challenges their sense of nascent greatness. Adults and young people do not understand each other. But instinctively most young people believe that God understands them. In that belief they pray. Doors open. They get help.

Adults who have known the arid barrenness of life in the "far country" and who have then turned back to God through Jesus Christ come into an exhilarating season of joyous experience in their new life. From contrite hearts they prayed for pardon and got it. They were born again. They became babes in Christ. As such they were given heavenly nurture. They prayed again; and, again, God heard and answered. They gave up their false self-sufficiency for the all-sufficiency of God.

Time passes. The first wondrous days of new life in Christ are now months or years in the past. The new birth brought permanent new values. It did not, however, give freedom from temptation. The same tempter who sought to seduce Jesus undertakes the seduction of every Christian. He is the one who first persuaded man to break away from God. Again and again he tempts, dangling the lure of a short cut to the attainment of selfishly desirable ends. He persuades with piously rationalized proposals. He promises self-merited blessings. The "Father, give me" motive of preborn-again days has a long hang-over in the life of nearly all Christians. The terms of their relationship to Christ become obscured in the revival of their self-centered desires. They know they should be the servants of the grace of Christ. He should always be cherished as Saviour, Lord, and Lawgiver. But still, they feel the tugging urge to reverse their status and pray,

> *Dear Lord:*
> *Please give me*
> *What I want,*
> *As I want it,*
> *When I want it.*

Even if not in these words, in this spirit and attitude they pray. God never answers a Christian's prayer born of such a motive.

Many, in the years after they have come to know Christ, become what might be described as hardened Christians. In spirit and attitude toward both God and men they are among the Pharisees and scribes of their own day. They are self-opinionated, self-righteous, and self-sufficient. In their ideas and actions they seem to expect the Word of God to agree with their interpretations. They are proud because they abstain from things which have never tempted them. In their vain self-appreciation they expect God to give them a dollar's worth of credit for a penny's worth of service. At the same time they are blind to the virtues of others. They represent the final status of those who persist to the ultimate in praying, "Father, give me."

The Christian Pharisee, however, is not typical. There is the temptation to say that he is not Christian at all. For most people God's discipline is effective, his protection against temptation freely accepted. I think I can honestly say that

God has not answered a single "Father, give me" prayer of mine in thirty-five years. Sometimes I have wondered why, and then I have realized that I was being disciplined, that I was being protected from myself.

As we develop in the Christian life, we should attain a measure of spiritual maturity. God helps us by providing the things we need and denying us those things which hinder our progress. His discipline helps us to grow in the graces of Christlikeness. If we accept it, if we trust him even when we disagree with him, we increase in the riches of his living fellowship. If we assert our own wills, we harden into a state of pharisaical self-righteousness. This is a fact each Christian needs to ponder. Everyone needs to ask himself, "Am I growing by the pattern of God's discipline for my life in Christ?"

Many times in the New Testament, Christians are called saints. In fact, the name "saint" is a synonym for Christian. At least twice, however, Paul uses the word with a slightly different meaning, giving us a clue to the processes of God's nurturing discipline. In Romans we read: "To all God's beloved in Rome, who are called to be [become] saints" (Rom. 1:7, RSV). The same expression is used in 1 Corinthians 1:2.

Most of us know that our salvation has three tenses: we have been saved; we are being saved; we shall be saved. The past refers to the primary regeneration which brought eternal life's initial experience. The present is one's continuing increase in Christ. All our days after conversion are involved in our becoming saints. But for too many, little growth is evident. Sometimes in order to be corrected, we have to be chastened severely. God's corrective discipline constrains us to press on the road to sainthood. If necessary, he employs drastic measures to stimulate our progress.

The future—we shall be saved—is prophetic of the final perfection of sanctification in Christ. This is the consummation of Christian blessedness to share in the ultimate glory of Christ in heaven.

As God disciplines the Christian to stimulate his increase in Christ, he stops answering "Father, give me" prayers. The youth in Christ finally reaches the stage at which his diet is no longer the spiritual baby food of former days. He gets very hungry and becomes conscious finally of spiritual starvation. In his need he has a real experience of crisis. He is bewildered. The Holy Spirit leads him back to the focus of that crisis of years before where, far from home in a strange land, it happened with him as it did with the prodigal.

One who has had this experience the second time knows it is nearly as difficult to go back to the Father with the same confession and prayer as it was the first time. Those who climb that mountain have learned the way to the treasure house of their Heavenly Father. They have learned that when God ceases to honor "Father, give me" prayers, it is in order that he may do something better. God wants his son in Christ to know that "Father, make me" prayers never fail to be wondrously answered. They are the golden ladder up which the helplessly dependent Christian who is becoming a saint climbs to satisfying communion with God.

4

Playing God

> *Not many days later, the younger son gathered all he had and took his journey into a far country, and there he squandered his property in loose living.*
>
> LUKE 15:13, RSV

Y NAME IS Ozymandias, king of kings:
Look on my works, ye Mighty, and despair!"
Nothing beside remains. Round the decay
Of that colossal wreck, boundless and bare
The lone and level sands stretch far away.

P. B. SHELLEY

Ozymandias was playing God. His vanity is universal; his delusion is the curse of all. Every man has said, "I am the master of my fate; I am the captain of my soul."

We have tried to prove it in many ways. Ozymandias built a statue. Cheops built a pyramid which was to guard his mummified immortality until beyond the very end of time. Prudent men place their faith in savings and pension funds; the daring carve out empires. The sin of it all is pride—the belief that I can determine my nature and destiny for myself in defiance of whatever gods and universes there may be.

You can see this sin most clearly in its innocent form—the dreams of childhood. During the early years, reality is not so insistent a companion as it will later become, and life is full of fantasies. Children invent playmates, situations, even whole worlds, and they move from one to the other, in and out of adult reality, with the ease of perfect innocence and freedom from limitation. All things are possible. Trolls and pixies can sit side by side with grandmothers in perfect comfort. The voices of the wind and woods speak with just as much meaning as the voices of parents.

By teen age these dreams lose some of their innocence. They become egocentric. The adventures of dreamland are no longer simple pleasure; they become instead a feeble compensation for some dreary, unheroic, real world which the dreamer is trying to escape. Dissatisfied with the world given him by God, the dreamer makes himself a new one nearer to his heart's desire. He feeds on the satisfactions of this fake world, nourishing illusions of personal grandeur, thinking of himself more highly than he ought to think, and building his personality on false foundations. His self-esteem is a lie.

We can laugh at the present-day Napoleons who spend their lives in padded cells. Their lie is an obvious one. Their delusion we can define as insanity. But all of us lie to ourselves. We grow with difficulty out of our childish ways. We have an exaggerated opinion of our importance. Christ would call us, as he called his own generation, "children sitting in the market places" (Matt. 11:16, RSV).

The innocence of childhood conceals another potential sin—impersonation. They call it "play-like"—like fathers and mothers, school teachers and students, cops and robbers, soldiers, preachers, brides and grooms. In every conceivable way, children try in their play to imitate adults. This is natural and good. Someday they will be adults, and they are only looking forward to their appointed future.

But Ozymandias was playing God, and this is a vastly different matter. God is omipotent, omnipresent, and self-sufficient. He thinks, dreams, imagines, and conceives—and worlds whirl into being. He ponders, and reality itself receives its definition. He acts, and moral law comes into being, patterned after the definitive goodness of his action. He wills, and all history is begun, continued, shaped, and concluded. God is reality and the cause of all reality. He can have no delusions of grandeur, because his grandeur is no illusion. It is a fact, the supreme fact of our universe.

When man's dreams reach out to grasp the grandeur of God and when his bent to impersonation presumes upon the nature of God, he has committed the archetype of all sin. The first man and woman in the garden gambled all they had in a venture to become gods themselves. They ate of the fruit of the tree that was in the midst of the garden in order that they might become like God, knowing good from evil. They hazarded God's favor in an effort to gain independence and self-sufficiency, and lost all, forever and for all posterity. But still we try, casting aside God's friendship in a vain effort to capture his throne. We deny God's sovereignty in our lives and assert instead our own. It was this sinful assertion that Jesus saw clearly in all the people he encountered. It was this that he described when he said of the prodigal, "Not many days later, the younger son gathered all he had and took his journey into a far country, and there he squandered his property in loose living." In these twenty-eight graphic words he records the spiritual life story of every man who lives his life independently of the mastery of God.

This sin is universal. "The whole world is in the power of the evil one" (1 John 5:19, RSV) . "The god of this world has blinded the minds of the unbelievers, to keep them from seeing the light of the gospel of the glory of Christ, who is the likeness of God" (2 Cor. 4:4 RSV) . "All have sinned and fall short of the glory of God" (Rom. 3:23, RSV) . "The imagination of man's heart is evil from his youth" (Gen. 8:21, RSV) . And "what will it profit a man, if he gains the whole world and forfeits his life?" (Matt. 16:26, RSV) .

When a person tries to play God, inevitably he fails. His statues crumble; his pyramids are rifled; his dreams fade. In the end, all that is left is the misery of sin, condemned and doomed under the judgment of Almighty God.

For the wrath of God is revealed from heaven against all ungodliness and wickedness of men who by their wickedness suppress the truth. For what can be known about God is plain to them, because God has shown it to them. Ever since the creation of the world his invisible nature, namely, his eternal power and deity, has been clearly perceived in the things that have been made. So they are without excuse; for although they knew God they did not honor him as God or give thanks to him, but they became futile in their thinking and their senseless minds were darkened. Claiming to be wise, they became fools, and exchanged the glory of the immortal God for images resembling mortal man or birds or animals or reptiles.

Therefore God gave them up in the lusts of their hearts to impurity, to the dishonoring of their bodies among themselves, because they exchanged the truth about God for a lie and worshiped and served the creature rather than the Creator, who is blessed forever! Amen (Rom. 1:18–24, RSV) .

Thus does the Bible describe the origin, growth, and ruinous end of man's universal adventure in trying to play God. We are all selfish, self-centered, egotistical, and conceited. In thousands of subtle ways we justify ourselves in our self-worship. I have even heard ministers use Christ's command to love our neighbors as ourselves to defend self-centeredness.

One of the principles of psychology is that there is a correlation between proper self-respect and respect for others. This is true and good. But the church can fairly well depend on it that most people are going to be able to cultivate self-respect without any help from anyone else. They don't need to be told, "Love yourself in order that then you may properly love your neighbor." Such a command, no matter how true it may be as a scientific description in psychology, is but an open invitation to Satan. It allows him to persuade Christians that they can be Christian and selfish at the same time.

And this is the danger. Man does not really set out to be deliberately wicked. He rather convinces himself that the wicked thing he wants to do is really good. Sin is deceptive. It lures man's mind with wondrously attractive fantasies. With a sin at a time man builds his self-confidence. Gradually he comes to believe that he really is strong, self-sufficient— even infallible. His desires become his definition of goodness, his will his moral law. Almost before he knows it, he has followed the track of pleasure, profit, and power into that doomed far country on the backside of God's will.

The Bible and the experience of man prove, to anyone willing to be honest with himself and his God, that Satan is pretty much the lord of this world—and as much of the next as he can get his hands on. Nevertheless, it seems to be fashionable in some circles to cast sophisticated doubt on the existence of Satan. The age of superstition is supposedly past, and evil spirits no longer inhabit every tree. Haunted houses can usually be rented, and family ghosts are reduced to fireside tales. Satan becomes a Miltonic fancy, interesting as fiction but hardly credible as fact. This is the age of science, and religion ought to be reasonable.

It is true that having to account for Satan often makes theologies and philosophies of history just a bit less logically neat than they otherwise would have been, but this is a small enough price to pay for the truth. The end of religion is not to provide the basis for a neat theology, nor even less to provide the Sunday morning amusement for a technological Never-Never Disneyland. The end of religion is to determine the nature and destiny of man. The fact of evil is central in our culture, whether we admit it or not. Two wars and constant rivalries seem to prove that modern man is living by at least one Christian doctrine to absolute perfection—the doctrine of original sin, of innate human perversity. The malevolent design and power of Satan have seemingly captured the minds and aspirations of men. Satan has seduced them into becoming his allies in challenging the authority of God, in denying the character of God as supreme good, and in attempting to achieve the self-sufficiency of God.

Throughout the Bible, and consequently in all of life, the character and purpose of God and the character and purpose of Satan stand out in striking opposition. God's compassionate desire is to save and bless all men. Satan's malicious scheme is to persuade every human being to disown and to dishonor God.

This is the conflict, and these are the only alternatives. Man's power of choice involves him irretrievably. There is no possibility of neutrality. From the very beginning of conscious life, if he is being reared in a Christian environment, his soul hears God's offer of eternal life. But just as insistent come the subtle suggestions of Satan, the gilded visions of the far country, that are as enticing as a feathered fly and just as barbed. According to the Bible, every human being from Adam and Eve to the present hour has made the prodigal's choice. Jesus knew this. His mission in the world was to rescue and redeem men from the consequences of this choice. He seeks to save them from the disasters that playing God inescapably brings.

In the parables of the fifteenth chapter of Luke, Jesus tries to show all men, dramatically and graphically, what is wrong. The young man who went into the far country stands for Everyman, for all mankind. Thus to learn about ourselves we look at him—at the young man who left home.

His name is John—or Isaac, or Ivan, Pierre or Pedro, Hans or Michael or Giovanni—the name really doesn't matter. He is all of them, and all of us. He may be tall or short, but he thinks himself attractive and wears his robe with as much grace as he can muster. There is a furrow in his brow and a dark look in his eyes. His mouth is ever so imperceptibly one-sided, in what could hardly be called a sneer, but which at least wells up from some deep dissatisfaction.

Like most of us, he is unappreciated. Nobody listens to his ideas or bows in genuine respect to greet him. His name is Bar-Something—"the son of." He has nothing of his own, nothing in his own right. He is merely the son of his father, a laborer in the family vineyard, the family wine press, the family sheepfold. Even worse, he is a younger son, deprived of the privileges which his lordly elder brother flaunts so proudly.

When he was younger, things were no better. For as long as he could remember he had been ordered about, regulated, told what to do and what to say and even sometimes what to think. The virtues of his elder brother were held up to him. His own small mistakes were magnified into deliberate sins. As he grew older and larger and stronger, even his father shrank in stature. He become less and less of a god and more and more a mere man, afflicted with increasingly old-fashioned notions. Many times the younger son had thought of running away from it all, but he could not, in the years of his childhood, bring himself to it. But as the years passed and he came into the beginning of adulthood, he increasingly found himself in conflict with his father and with everything his father represented. He had a compulsive desire to escape authority. Restraint irritated him. He became more and more self-confident, until he convinced himself that he was absolutely right in his resentments and desires. More and more he wanted to break away, but he did not want to go empty-handed. Finally, he made his decision and prayed his fatal prayer: "Father, give me."

There comes a time when fathers can no longer protect their children from themselves. The younger son got what he wanted, even though the father knew that he was measuring out with every shekel responsibility the boy could not manage.

Authority is a paradoxical thing, hated and loved in turn by all mankind. There has never lived a child who has not been a rebel. The universe is not heliocentric or geocentric. It is egocentric. I am the center of my universe. When I have planned a picnic, I take the afternoon shower as a personal affront. When I am waiting in line, those ahead of me are insufferably slow, but when it is my turn, I take all the time I think I need. Gates with "No Admittance" signs beckon to my explorer's instinct, a wet-paint notice brings forth my testing finger, and watermelons always taste sweetest when stolen.

Wise parents know that they should try to use as few prohibitions as possible because each one is but an open invitation to disobedience. But absolute freedom from authority is absolute disaster. Imagine a man without family, without nationality, without religion, without a personal past, living in a world which contains only him. He is free to do exactly as he pleases, but he doesn't really have anything worth doing to do. He is nothing. He needs authority.

This the younger son did not know. He got what he wanted —unrestricted freedom and money to pay for his fancies. He thought these would be enough, but he was tragically mistaken. What he did not know that is true stands in startling contrast with the much that he knew that is not so. He did not realize that he thought he was smarter than God.

He could not see that he was kicking away the ladder up which he had climbed to the best that there was in his life. It had not entered his mind that greatness could not be cheaply bought. He did not know that even if he could achieve a measure of success, it would be filled with tragedy without his father's presence to bless it. It never occurred to him that if gifts from others are to bless, the givers must be respected.

Not once did he perceive that playing God is a destroying madness. He had seen others fall, but he never dreamed that he would fall. The illusion of sin is a heady wine that intoxicates its drinker with a sense of invincibility. His dreams of glory turned into shimmering realities just over the horizon. Though dreams had led others only to a grave, this man would be different. He would succeed. All he had to do was go to the far country, that magical far-off place that had never heard of his father, that would place no restrictions on him, and that would respect him as the man of property that he really was. He had seen from afar the sudden riches of the gaming tables and the opulence of speculative fortune, and he could feel the gold of that far-off country already pouring into his hands, heavy in his purse. He did not really want something for nothing—he only wanted what he thought a person of his merit deserved. He had not sold his soul to Satan—not in so many words. But he was quite willing to use

Satan as his broker, confident that he could take a profit and get out without being burned. He was smart. He was shrewd. He would show these doddering old provincials who couldn't see beyond the fence of his father's farm that there was more to the world than they had ever dreamed.

He never realized that the far country with the golden rooftops is no longer a far country when you go to it, or that what looks like gold in the glory of a distant sunset often turns out to be but yellow tile and tarnished brass. Far countries always turn out more and more like home the longer you stay there. People are people the world over. If they cut your throat on Wall Street, they will skin you alive in Hong Kong. If they don't appreciate you in Podunk where they know you, they certainly won't appreciate you in Paris where they never saw you before. At home the younger son was at least the son of his father, respected at least in a reflected light. In the far country he was only a foreign yokel ripe for fleecing.

He was a fool, of course. No one, least of all a younger son, can roll the universe into his own private little ball and then hurl it into orbit around himself. The attempt is playing God—a thing doomed by definition. Like the puppet show, the God-player may put up a fair appearance for a little while, but when the person who pulls the strings walks out on stage, the illusion is forever destroyed. And the Almighty God is always present on every stage, even though prodigals are at times too blind to see him.

Tragically, we are all blind at times. In all the generations of man, every one of us is a God-player. Until the shocks come, every one of us feels self-sufficient; we are self-sufficient because of wealth, intelligence, family, connections, prestige, physical strength—all the worldly things that man is slave to. In one of his farewell addresses to the children of Israel Moses recognized this fact and warned the people:

Take heed lest you forget the Lord your God, by not keeping his commandments . . . lest, when you have eaten and are full, and have built goodly houses and live in them, . . . then your heart be lifted up, and you forget the Lord your God, . . . Beware lest you say in your heart, 'My power and the might of my hand have gotten me this wealth.' . . . And if you forget the Lord your God and go after other gods . . . I solemnly warn you this day that you shall surely perish. . . . because you would not obey the voice of the Lord your God (Deut. 8:11–12,14,17–20, RSV).

But men never listen. Heedless of the compassionate love of God, men break away from him. They serve their own selfish pleasures under the delusion that they do not need God. They make their choice to become the worshipers of Mammon, the slaves of Satan. In all generations they have found it easier to believe the complimentary lies of Satan than the harsh but redemptive truths of God. Choosing Satan, they begin to travel the road toward the disaster which overwhelmed the prodigal. Most of them have to go all the way there before God can bring them to their senses. For most men, only the shock of total despair can open their souls to God's grace and serve as the beginning of wisdom.

In this world the hardest thing we have to learn is the truth about ourselves. By nature we tend always to think well of ourselves. Regardless of what happens, we are never to blame. What we do is always right and worthy of praise. We magnify our achievements and forget about our failures. When crises come, we timidly turn our backs, think as positively as we can, and hope that our troubles will go away. If we succeed, we credit our magnificent ability and persevering hard work. If we fail, we say we didn't get the breaks. Christ's way of humility in service is changed, sometimes even in the churches, into the way of self-glorification and acquisition. If Christ were to return, preaching his gospel of peace, modern Pharisees would burn him at a heretic's stake. They would have no choice. Christ would be upsetting. When man is playing God, there is no room anywhere for a real God.

The God-players of this generation wear many faces. Like the prodigal, they have thought themselves sufficient, not in need of any God. But unlike the prodigal, they are not so blatant about it. Our generation has no Pharaohs, no Caesars, no men who say in so many blasphemous words: "I am God. Worship me." Few men are willing to say with Louis XIV, "The state, it is myself." Modern God-players are gregarious. They go to hell as individuals, but they make their gods as groups. Instead of deifying themselves, they deify their creations, their organizations, their theories, their causes. Man is scientifically omnipotent; we will therefore worship man. We will worship him by worshiping the Atomic Energy Commission. We will worship him by selling our souls to General Motors. We will worship him by selling our lives to the installment plan. We will worship him by selling our churches to statistical goals.

It is all very well to condemn the Marxists for elevating material progress and state socialism into the very throne of the Almighty. Such God-playing denies the spiritual nature of man, flaunts the very foundations of our faith, and leads inevitably to the most total slavery this world has ever seen. But it is not enough to condemn Moloch and Dagon, the gods of the enemy. We must also admit that we have set up Baals in our own houses.

It is a strange paradox that the nation which above all others in this world proclaims the spiritual values of a free democracy should be the nation whose material prosperity is its greatest achievement and most revered divinity. It is a paradox that the nation of rugged individualists has so joyously adopted the new way of life of the "organization man" and deified the amorphous standards of the anonymous group. It is a paradox that the nation of Jonathan Edwards and George Whitefield has become a place where church meeting houses can be referred to as "plants." It is a paradox that the nation founded under God, "with liberty and justice for all," has made its material products its God, its human theories its Bible, and whatever its citizens approve its morality. This is the paradoxical but ruinous disaster that comes from playing God.

Sooner or later the long finger of God will prick the balloon of man's overweening self-esteem. He has never failed throughout the long record of history and the Bible. Tyrants, devils, popes, false prophets—all find that their assumed divinity is but for the moment.

> He who sits in the heavens laughs;
>   the Lord has them in derision.
> Then he will speak to them in his wrath,
>   and terrify them in his fury, saying,
> "I have set my king
>   on Zion, my holy hill."
> . . . .
> "You shall break them with a rod of iron,
>   and dash them in pieces like a potter's vessel."
>   PSALM 2:4–6,9, RSV

The long finger of God finally overtakes the soul that is running away. The divine finger of revelation and judgment brings a fugitive from God to the consciousness of his woeful want. In the crisis of decision the fugitive turns and by the grace of God sets his face toward heaven.

Or he ignores despair and plods stubbornly and wilfully on to hell.

5

The Inescapable End

> *And when he had spent everything, a great famine arose in that country, and he began to be in want. So he went and joined himself to one of the citizens of that country, who sent him into his fields to feed swine. And he would gladly have fed on the pods that the swine ate; and no one gave him anything.*
>
> LUKE 15:14–16, RSV

I HAVE SEEN the moment of my greatness flicker,
And I have seen the eternal Footman
   hold my coat, and snicker,
And in short, I was afraid.*

Eventually the end comes to all vanities, all merely human greatnesses. There is left for unbelievers only the sardonic laugh of death, as he helps them on with the coat they wear as they leave this house party called life. For thousands of years God and human experience have taught that reaping what one has sown is the inescapable end of all men. Thus do all who never return to God.

---

* From *Collected Poems*, 1909–1935, by T. S. Eliot, copyright 1936 by Harcourt, Brace and Company, Inc. and reprinted with their permission.

47

Thus did the prodigal. His money was gone. He had sown vanity; he reaped emptiness. His wild oats had ripened into famine, his purchased friends into grunting swine.

More tragic still, he had invested in this worthless crop everything he had. He had spent his all. He had spent his money, his inheritance; but he had spent far more than this. Men have things other than money to spend. Certainly we spend time, the fruits of mind and soul, and the assets of character and the spirit. Unless a man invests life's most valuable resources in ways that can enhance them, he is doomed one day to find himself in the depths of moral and spiritual bankruptcy. Such is the inescapable end of all who maintain their revolt against God and depend upon an exalted concept of themselves.

Jesus saw all this that day when he and the group of publicans and sinners and Pharisees and scribes met at the same time and in the same place. The Saviour was always interested in every aspect of a man's life. He was concerned for the sick, the maimed, the hungry, the socially condemned, the morally perverted, and those deceived by self-righteousness. Beyond these important essentials he clearly perceived the immortality of the human spirit, the conscious personality that would never cease its existence. His soul was heavily weighted with concern because of the spiritual peril that surrounded all persons whom he met. He knew that regardless of how far into sin they had gone, they could be saved. He could redeem them. They could be born again; blessed deliverance from their condemnation could be theirs.

Jesus knew that unless sinners became aware of themselves and their sin, they would all eternally perish. His mission in the world was to meet men and women in all the hours and circumstances of life and minister to them in every need. In these verses Jesus is telling us that spenders must face want.

This is a lesson that God has written in large letters in many places for all men to read. He has graphically reinforced it with tragic illustrations. Regardless of where we have lived or what our circumstances may have been, we have seen those who "had spent everything." People are tested most severely in the area of their spending. More people know how to earn than know how to spend. This principle has many applications.

We easily think of its relevance to money. Two brothers who were skilled craftsmen with good jobs had a sister who was in her first year of teaching school. Their parents died in an accident. Nearly a hundred thousand dollars was divided among them. Each quit his job. In two years they had spent all their money. But this was not all. They had so wasted their reputations, neglected their talents, and scorned their true friends that none of them was qualified to resume earning a living with anything like the ability he had before the binge.

Fourteen millionaires in 1929 had their offices in the same building. In 1932 each was financially a pauper. Another man's salary rapidly increased. But with every increase he and his wife increased their spending out of proportion to the salary boost. Their folly overtook them with disastrous results. Jesus is telling us here that financial wastrels cannot escape the debacle which their folly creates.

In every community there are those who, long before they are old, have spent their physical resources. Tom Brown at twenty gave promise of being the greatest athlete the county had ever produced, but at thirty-two he was a semi-invalid because he had senselessly overspent. Millions of people have proved that physical wastrels cannot escape the hurt—in sickness, pain, and weakness—that their foolish spending produces.

The moral paupers in every community prove the frightful price that some seem willing to pay for pleasure. Their prize is an evil mess of dishonorable pottage, and for it they are willing to pay to the last poor pence of decency. They make a god of passion, an altar of lust, and a sacrifice of their own bodies and souls. Their end is remorse, loneliness, and terror.

Society is sick with the parasites who are willing to spend their integrity for gain. They may be the shiftless beggars who so much enjoy an easy living that they are willing to cringe and whine for it, accepting the scraps thrown by disgusted pity and gradually melting away every vestige of the backbone of their souls. Worse are the bloated rich who garner their worldly goods by every sort of expediency, even when in hypocrisy they try to bribe society with scholarships for the most deserving of orphans. Worse still are the rich who aren't yet bloated but who would like to be and who haven't time even for hypocrisy. Their only morality is the furtherest stretch of the law—the appearance demanded by the bought congressman or the chattel sheriff. They are expense-account rich. They have no loyalties. They neglect their children. They decorate their homes with a succession of wives. The only truth they recognize is the price tag, and even this is adjustable. But even the most depraved of them are not immune to the bankruptcy of spirit that grows with their riches and at the last overwhelms them.

Jesus understood all these people. He knew that their trouble was that they were spiritual rebels against God; that whatever the form of their action, they were at heart spiritual wastrels, trying to achieve success by playing God. They were throwing away their true inheritance, seeking instead the tinsel riches of Satan's palace of illusion. They may have been publicans and sinners, seeking material wealth or carnal pleasure. They may have been scribes and

Pharisees, revelling in arrogance and spiritual pride. Whatever their category, they were spiritual wastrels.

And they include all mankind. In some measure and to some degree we have all been wastrels and would be still but for the grace of God in Jesus Christ that has saved us. Multiplied millions of people have never experienced this grace. They are in continued rebellion against the light that God has shined upon their path. They have permitted themselves to be beguiled by the god of this world into the quest of his delusions.

For these and all such there come the days of great famine and bitter want.

Anyone who has watched life for very long learns to recognize the phenomenon which can be called the sequence of disaster. At first, credit of all kinds is easy to get. Devils have an unlimited expense account; they can take their victims for very plush rides. When a man has resources, while some of his inheritance of wealth or talent or reputation is still left, many friends are eager to be helpful and kind. They sell him the wine that creates illusions of grandeur. They peddle him the narcotics that make him a slave of his desires. By flattery they intoxicate his vanity until he is sure that he is of all men most superior. But his spending is always just a bit greater than his income, and eventually all is consumed. Then Satan's salesmen cease to smile and entertain and become his bill collectors. They no longer extend easy credit, easy terms. Suddenly a man finds himself stranded with nothing. His thirst becomes torture; his hunger for narcotic illusions shakes him into ghastly deliriums. He is harried with demands for payment. A bankrupt debtor, he is bedeviled to desperation. Eventually he reaches the despair of the prodigal.

This despair is the inevitable destination of all who persist in going away from God. It is a place of bitter winter for the soul, a place of total famine. With a few telling words Jesus said all that God and human experience needs to say to describe the unutterable tragedy that suddenly seizes the spiritual wastrel. Once the poor sinner finds himself broke from trying to buy himself rich in the devil's market place, he becomes suddenly aware of terrible trouble. While the roof is crashing in on his head, the floor is falling out from under his feet to drop him deeper into the pit. Then the debris gives him the final blow. Selfish, evil living and excesses of various kinds have gained him no friends. He finds himself left with enfeebled powers to meet the tragic crises that have assailed him. His defeated self-competence is ill-prepared to sustain him in the shock that has overtaken him. Forfeiting his self-respect has, without his realizing it, destroyed his abilities to engineer a successful recovery. He is like one awakening out of a terrifying nightmare only to find that the reality of his disaster exceeds the terror of his dream. Instantly he determines to do something about it. Every time he gets up and tries to make a new start, frustration flattens him at a level lower than where he started. Then he hits the bottom.

To understand the agony the prodigal suffered in his last desperate effort to prevent physical starvation we need to remember that those to whom Jesus told that story were Jews. The citizen of that country to whom the prodigal went and joined himself was a Gentile. All the work that he could give the boy to do, or would give him to do, or for which he might remotely have ability, was to take care of the swine. For those Jews who heard this story, no degradation could be deeper. In stating it as he did, Jesus was graphically portraying, beyond anything most of our minds have caught, the unspeakable humiliation, helplessness, and hopelessness that forsaking God ultimately brings.

This was the most horrible spiritual hell that could ever befall a halfway decent Jew of that day. To work for a Gentile was bad enough, but to feed pigs was even worse. To be forced by need into begging, thievery, or even prostitution would not be so painful to one of us as was this ultimate degradation to a pious Jew of Jesus' day. This is the inevitable end of those who run away from God and try to be God for themselves. He who soars thus on wings of godless self-will inescapably exhausts his strength somewhere in the midst of his flight. Suddenly he is falling deep into chasms below his starting point, where he is shattered on the hard, flinty rocks of reality.

Jesus very precisely described what happened to the prodigal. "He went and joined himself to one of the citizens of that country." It could have been Rome, Alexandria, Corinth, or Ephesus. It could easily have been that this citizen was one of the men who had helped to swindle the prodigal out of his fortune. Such men have often given their victims miserable employment to save them from starvation. Even the devil sometimes seems to be so ashamed that he makes a slight gesture at salving his conscience.

Sin and its results can be terribly ironic. Until the regenerating power of God's redeeming grace works the miracle of new spiritual birth in a sinner, one of the frequent consequences of sin is its disabling effect upon his abilities. Perhaps one of the things Jesus meant to portray in this picture is that the young man's sin had wrought a degeneration of his abilities until he was no longer capable of better employment. Such a thing happens often. In every city one can find those who once were highly gifted and whose skills were much desired until sin deteriorated them into unemployable incompetents.

Could any contrast be more pathetic than that between

the situation of this man when he was living with his father and when Jesus said of him, "He would gladly have fed on the pods [carob beans] that the swine ate." The deadliness of sin in perverting man's thinking, debasing his situation, and degrading his personality has never been so vividly described as this sentence presents it. These words eat like acid into our imaginations when we come to recognize what Jesus saw. He saw a man, created in the image of his Father God, who possessed all the blessed potentials that God's love and purpose was eager to bestow upon him, who had foolishly claimed riches he had not earned, and who, despising the God who had made him, believed the god of this world and so far corrupted his character, appetite, and desire that the diet of hogs seemed to him delectable. Alas, it is a true picture.

The final brush stroke to complete this part of the picture is done with six words: "And no man gave him anything." In the beginning God had given this son everything. He pressed on in rebellion until the fortune he had inherited had been dissipated. One might easily miss the point that Jesus is making here. Basically, however, do we not have here a profoundly significant thing? We can never see it if we simply think of this as a story that Jesus happened to tell, but whenever we face the fact that Jesus is painting the spiritual biography of every sinful soul, then how could these words mean anything else than this: "No man was able to give him anything." The sickness, the hunger, the thirst, the hurt, and the poverty of sinners who have come to the end of their road cannot be met by anything that mere man can bestow. We have no human resources that can supply such need. The only one who is competent is God.

6

Self-awareness

But when he came to himself . . .
LUKE 15:17, RSV

I<small>T</small> <small>HAS BEEN SAID</small> that the sciences have developed in inverse relation to their nearness to man's life. The human quest for knowledge seems to have first focused on the heavens. In a sense, astronomy is that which is furtherest removed from man's consciousness of himself. The natural sciences—geology, chemistry, physics, biology, and botany—have fascinated human interest. Psychology, the scientific study of human personality and the reasons for its behavior, was in a very real sense the last of the sciences to be born. Man is far more willing to put objective reality into a test tube than he is to get in himself and seek the knowledge that would enable him to evaluate and discipline himself correctly.

Is it not measurably correct to say that the most baffling problem with which men have to deal is the mystery of themselves? How many of us can explain satisfactorily to ourselves why we do much that we do? Not many of us know enough of that mysterious stranger, the "I" within the more familiar

"Me." In the seventh chapter of Romans the apostle Paul described the experience of every man. "I do not understand my own actions. For I do not do what I want, but I do the very thing I hate" (Rom. 7:15, RSV). Not many of us have developed a satisfactory explanation for what the apostle described. What he said is a true account of our experience over the years. It is this lack of the understanding of ourselves that keeps many people in a state of bewildered confusion. The better thing to recall is that no man has found the answer to all the questions his experiences raise.

Beyond, however, lies the great fact that God does know and understand. Jesus knew that in all of us there are elements of divinity and iniquity. Each element is striving for mastery. The purpose of his coming into the world was to enable those who accepted his redemptive lordship to win the final victory in this life-and-death struggle. It was to help us understand this that he painted the picture in this parable.

Jesus knew that men would never seek salvation until they had become conscious of their need. In the experience of the prodigal Jesus shows us the crisis which comes to people in that far country away from God. The prodigal's despairing need and helpless hopelessness opened the channels of his thinking to remember his father. It is from such hours of crisis that souls turn back to God or, alas, stumble on to hell.

There is, however, more to the parable than this. The journey into the far country is more than just a journey into hell. The crisis is not only the experience of conviction that leads an unbeliever to salvation or damnation. The prodigal also can represent the Christian as well as the sinner.

Many people receive Jesus Christ as their Saviour and Lord in early childhood. They never make the wanton break away from the Father God, as did the young man in Jesus' story. They have the better way, the way that Jesus in his concern for children wanted them to have. Long before sin has corrupted, wasted, and dishonored them, they embrace Jesus as Saviour and are delivered from the wantonness of original depravity. Jesus met them through Christian fathers and mothers and through the pastors and teachers of the church. He brought them to a knowledge of himself before in self-will they tried to run away from God. They never squandered their spiritual inheritance, as older youth and adults frequently and tragically do. Those who receive Jesus before they have had time to become wilful runaways are delivered from great suffering. They are never cursed with the experience that brings a Christless soul to himself.

The life of a Christian, however, has analogous crises. Those who commit themselves to Christ before they have deliberately turned their backs on God may in later years come under the power of Satan's beguiling persuasion and journey into the far country. They will have their fling at playing God, but one thing is certain: those who have actually experienced the new birth in Christ will, like Peter after he denied his Lord, eventually come to themselves and, as did he, go out and weep bitterly and turn back to Christ.

Some of those who go into far countries are neither physical, financial, nor social failures. By worldly standards they are persons of integrity and of the highest respectability. By the standards of human society they are not sick; neither are they blind. Spiritually, however, they are sick unto death and blind to their condition and fate. Their plight can finally become as desperate as that of the younger son when he had spent all. They, like him, have gotten themselves into the far country of the soul away from God. Their situation may be more dangerous than that of the prodigal. His disasters convinced him of his guilt and need. Their success has a tendency to give them the illusion of security. The sinner who is respectable from the human point of view frequently is the most difficult to awaken to his true condition. Here again, however, the long finger of the omnipotent God reaches out to make him aware of his real insecurity. God will not suffer any sinner to go to an eternal doom without thoroughly awakening him to his need. He will have to make life's supreme decision—the choice of eternal destiny.

The Pharisees and scribes were certainly strangers to the kind of wickedness that afflicted the publicans and sinners. They had not sat in the seat of the publican, nor had they felt the shame of the sinner. The sins of the others were beyond their comprehension. But they also suffered from a sin. They had an exaggerated conception of the iniquity of blatant sinners and just as exaggerated a conception of their own righteousness and spiritual wisdom. Because they loathed publicans and sinners, they were sure that God loathed them also. Jesus, therefore, could not possibly be the Messiah of God, because he did not have perception enough to recognize despicable people when he saw them. What is more, he seemed unable to appreciate their own shining righteousness. But they were deluded. They had made God into the image of their own self-righteousness. The publicans and sinners were sinners indeed, and they knew it. But the Pharisees and scribes were sinners, also, with this difference: They had called their sinning righteousness. In their self-justifying conceit they sat in judgment on both God and other men.

Jesus had warned them. In the Sermon on the Mount he admonished men not to judge others lest they condemn one for having a speck in his eye while they were blind to the stick that had destroyed their own vision. At another time Jesus warned the same people that many others, of whom they had a very small opinion, would in the great final judgment go into the kingdom ahead of them. And on another day he said to this same group, "Verily I say unto you, except ye repent, ye shall all likewise perish."

These are the people who take the journey into the far country and never realize the disaster they are in. One of them was the elder brother. He never left his home. In appearance he remained loyal. But his heart was in a spiritual far country more depraved and more hopeless than the one which ruined the prodigal. The elder brother was worse because he never came to himself. Such people seldom do. Their hardened shell of self-conceit is largely impervious to the startling forces which try to crack it. Their self-esteem immunizes them from any consciousness of their sinful unworthiness.

But despair and self-awareness eventually come to all who are willing to be honest with themselves and with God. Whether they are in the far country of pride and original sin or in the far country of backslidden failure, God will tell them the truth if they will listen. Satan would much prefer that all sinners be Pharisees because they are the easiest people to hold. But sometimes Satan overplays his hand. In many instances those whom he beguiles do not disgrace him. But some sink into such depths of depravity that they prove beyond any doubt that they are the devil's loathsome bums. Gangrene of the soul becomes as obvious as cancer of the reputation or as galloping consumption of the body. Such sinners have gone even beyond the designs of their deceiver. His satanic purpose is to destroy man's spiritual loyalty to God without making him a ghastly spectacle of iniquity. For often, when sin becomes such a horror, even the sinner can see it.

It is a shocking experience for one to see himself clearly

after he has long been the slave of sinful delusions. This discovery brings a series of startling revelations. To the sinner it is like traveling out of a long night that had been filled with delightful dreams only to be awakened by torturing nightmares. The agony of reality's full light falls upon him. For the first time since his childhood he recognizes himself for what he is. He has come to himself. Sin's illusions have vanished. He sees stark, terrible reality. He has become aware of his folly, stupidity, perversion, selfishness, and degradation. At last he knows the truth about himself. He had become the devil's dupe, the devil's slave.

The second startling discovery of the disillusioned sinner is the maliciousness of Satan. Jesus described it when he said, "The thief comes only to steal and kill and destroy" (John 10:10, RSV). The thief is Satan. In all his plans regarding man he has the same program. From it he never deviates. He desires to steal from every man his confidence in God, his belief in God's honesty, and his concept of what is good for himself. He fills a man's heart with ambitions. But he delivers only delusions that end in defeat and death. Satan has determined to kill a man's respect for righteousness, his sense of responsibility for himself, the fear of the consequences of his choice, and his respect for his divine inheritance. These designs are progressive and cumulative. Ultimately the god of this world aims to destroy within man the resources, elements, and qualities of his divine inheritance.

When a sinner genuinely comes to himself, he realizes that his personal guilt is a terrible fact. He has brought upon himself the condemnation of his own conscience. This recognition fills him with utter wretchedness and self-loathing. But though for a time this new knowledge is an unspeakably trying ordeal, it can be the last step through what seems to be a futile nightmare and into the dawn of life's best morning.

In such a crisis the Holy Spirit sets the facts of life in their true perspective. The sinner beholds and recognizes the actual depravity of his heart. His disillusionment opens his eyes to the truth about God and himself. He becomes aware of the privileges that he had forfeited. These recognitions are necessary to his deliverance.

When Saul of Tarsus was stricken as he neared Damascus, he was overwhelmed by the fearful depths into which his wrong thinking had cast him. He was a Pharisee of the Pharisees. He had been playing God in a highhanded way. People either had to accept his ideas of religion or die. Too many religious people have thought as he thought, but neither he nor they could get beyond the authority of the God and Father of our Lord and Saviour, Jesus Christ. Whether their degradation be the consequence of covetousness, dissipation, dishonesty, or the sins of decent men whose pride and self-esteem unseat God in their hearts, at some time before death they cannot escape a face-to-face meeting with God.

God employs a variety of ways or circumstances to bring a sinner to confront himself. Sometimes they are dramatic. In other instances the sinner sees what happens to others and such a warning brings him to think on his ways. Frustrating failures may become the instruments that move one to re-examine himself. Not a few finally begin to compare themselves with real Christians whom they have known. They discover that they have missed what others have found. Of this one can be certain—God will not let a sinner go to his final condemnation without seeking to turn him away from his doom. At various times in life and under varying circumstances the sinner will find his thoughts disturbed.

Usually the long hand of God opens the door to the sinner's self-discovery at the spot where he is most sensitive. It is the point where that man's resistance is weakest. It is the situation where his sense of need is greatest. It does not matter with God by what door he enters the human soul to bring that person face-to-face with reality about self, sin, and salvation. Once God has accomplished this in the human soul, the time of decision is near.

The prodigal stood amid the shambles of personal disaster. However, the urgency of his physical hunger was not his greatest hurt. It was his discovery of what he had done and become. He was a ghastly failure. Worse still, he had proved himself to have been a sinner. The self-esteem which had been his chief source of glory now made him ridiculous in his own eyes.

Men may run far from God, but they cannot escape him. Men try to escape him by utterly absorbing themselves in the interests that captivate their desires. Some refuse to allow themselves to think about God, to read anything that would turn their thoughts toward him, or to associate with those who might remind them of him. Some seek escape through drink. Hundreds of thousands drink themselves to unconsciousness every night so that they may have a few hours respite from fears that trouble them. Others frantically devise spiritual opiates of various kinds to give them some bit of tranquilizing relief from that deep inner awareness that there is an issue between them and the eternal God.

But ultimately there is no escape. Francis Thompson said:

> I fled Him, down the nights and down the days;
> I fled Him, down the arches of the years;
> I fled Him, down the labyrinthine ways
> Of my own mind; and in the mist of tears
> I hid from Him, and under running laughter.
> Up vistaed hopes, I sped;
> And shot, precipitated
> Adown Titanic glooms of chasmèd fears,

From those strong Feet that followed, followed after.
But with unhurrying chase,
And unperturbèd pace,
Deliberate speed, majestic instancy,
They beat—and a Voice beat
More instant than the Feet—
"All things betray thee, who betrayest Me."

Thus does God always pursue his own; thus far does his knowledge and presence extend. He is the "hound of heaven," he is the omnipresent one, he is the hunter who cannot be deceived, the arrow that cannot be outrun, the net that cannot be avoided or cut.

Yet his pursuit is the chase of love. God follows that he may redeem. He sends his Christ, the magnificently full revelation of his incarnate love, that men in seeing him might know the presence of God and allow the grace of God to create them anew.

Sin very definitely creates duality in human nature. Jesus knew this. There is within our being something that hungers for God. There is also a thirst for the bitter waters of sin that our perverted taste calls sweet. We are constantly pulled in two directions. This fact is strikingly illustrated in the struggle of the two Jacobs, the two Josephs, the two Davids, the Simon who became Peter, and the Saul of Tarsus who became Paul, the valiant apostle of Christ.

When a man comes to himself, he discovers this desperately perverted nature in control. Jesus knew from his own experience the pressure of Satan's persuasion. Through Satan's temptations our Saviour became perfected. He understands our need. His experience opened the springs of his holy compassion for sinners who yield where he won. That is the reason he made it so plain in the parable: As soon as one really comes to himself, he can arise and go to his father.

7

The Father's Other Son

Now his elder son was in the field;
and as he came and drew near to the
house, he heard music and dancing.
And he called one of the servants and
asked what this meant. And he said
to him, "Your brother has come, and
your father has killed the fatted calf,
because he has received him safe and
sound." But he was angry and refused
to go in. His father came out and en-
treated him, but he answered his fa-
ther, "Lo, these many years I have
served you, and I never disobeyed
your command . . ."

LUKE 15:25–32, RSV

THE LAST TEMPTATION is the greatest
    treason:
To do the right deed for the wrong reason.*

Jesus made it plain that to hunger and thirst after righteousness in order to be self-righteous, to preach the word of

* From "Murder in the Cathedral" by T. S. Eliot, copyright 1935 by Harcourt, Brace and Company, Inc. and reprinted with their permission.

God with power because it pleases one to be powerful, to have humility in order to be proud of it—these things are the greatest treason. The sins of the publican are great, but the sins of the Pharisee are great also. Christ's parable about a prodigal son has been taken as a parable about a sinner, and so it is. But it is also a parable about a Pharisee who is a sinner. Just as the younger son is the archetype of all men who rebel and come to themselves, so the elder brother is the archetype of all men whose souls become frozen in the sin of self-righteousness.

Christ was not merely reproving the prodigal publicans in his parable. He was addressing his total audience. He meant to reprove the sin of self-righteousness as much as the sin of immorality. But the reproof was not effective to all. The publicans and sinners drew near to hear him, and when they had heard him, they heeded him. The scribes and Pharisees heard him, heckled him, hated him, and finally planned his crucifixion.

From opposite motives these two groups came to talk with Jesus. The first were sinners. They knew what they were and wanted help. The second group were also sinners, but they thought themselves supremely righteous. The publicans and sinners were seeking a saviour to pardon their sin. Their critics, the haughty religious aristocrats, were scorning the Saviour and accusing him of sin.

In the parable the younger son, whose prototype was the publicans and sinners, confessed, "I have sinned." The elder brother, who was the prototype of the Pharisees and scribes, complained against his father, "Thou never gavest me." But Jesus had specifically said that "he divided his living between them."

These sinners were ready to pray the second prayer, but the hearts of the Pharisees were filled with murderous hatred for the only One who could save them. Saul of Tarsus is their archetype. Before the Damascus road meeting he was representative of the scribes and Pharisees in all their conflict with Jesus. Those who appear in the Gospels have the stage before the Lord's death and resurrection. Saul took the spotlight as the leader of their party after the ascension of Jesus. He had much of the responsibility for the deadly persecution of Christians. The hardest person in the world for God to tell anything is the man whose religion has given him a closed mind. It is not only closed but perverted into the delusion that God is obliged to agree with his views. So it had been with the Pharisees and with Saul.

But Saul was destined for nobler things. The Holy Spirit would not let him forget the dying Stephen. Try as ever he might on that journey to Damascus, again and again he remembered the voice, words, and spiritually transfigured countenance of the first deacon who died for Christ. His inability to ignore Stephen and the implications of his words and death built up terrific tensions inside his soul. They erupted into a prostrating crisis. Suddenly he was lying prone on the ground and heard a voice crying out of heaven, "Saul, Saul, why do you persecute me?"

The effect of this contrast is clear. It is not so difficult for those who are aware that they are lost to recognize their need of a saviour. It is much more difficult for Pharisees to come to a sense of guilt. They have built for themselves a personal salvation shelter whose foundation rests upon the sinking sands of their conceit, self-righteousness, and false religious ideas. They believe that God has to be as they think him to be. This is the spiritual peril of every soul that justifies himself before God.

In the parable of the two brothers Jesus is telling us that sin ultimately brings the sinner who is unrepentant and will not confess to a crisis. This fact creates an issue that multitudes of people through the centuries have sought to dodge when they were confronted with the gospel of Christ. Today an amazingly large percentage of those who regard themselves as Christians have tried to develop for themselves some detours around Christ's narrow gate into the kingdom of God.

Thus Jesus had a double audience. It was for this reason that he told his parable as he did, with its opening statement: "There was a man who had two sons" (Luke 15:11, RSV).

These two men were children of the same father. Here Jesus was affirming that publicans and sinners were created in the image of God, just as were scribes and Pharisees. Every man begins life with the same spiritual inheritance from God, the Creator. Any differences that develop come after the stamp of the divine image has been impressed.

These brothers were reared in the same home. One of the great mysteries of life is why brothers can be such opposites. Years ago I met a pastoral colleague who was troubled. He and his wife had two sons. When they were about twelve and fourteen years old, he told me that the older boy thought right and had the right attitudes and the right aspirations, but that the younger boy was the complete opposite. He said the younger one gravitated to what was wrong as water flows downhill. Now, twenty-five years after that conversation, the older boy is a great Christian leader and the younger brother is in the state penitentiary under a life sentence.

The impelling compulsions that dominate human personality are a mystery. Side by side the orange tree and the fatal hemlock grow and bear their fruit. One is a tree of life, the other a tree of death. Each thrusts its roots into the same soil and lifts its branches into the same air. One selects the elements that make it a benediction; the other chooses the poisons that make it deadly. It is here that human choice, insight, understanding, and responsibility have their critical crossroads.

Each of these sons had the same problem—sin. The tempter is no respecter of persons. Every newborn child is a challenge to Satan's authority. All the men and women who have ever lived have been tempted by the tempter and have become his subjects. Jesus emphatically declared: "Truly, truly, I say to you, unless one is born anew, he cannot see the kingdom of God" (John 3:3, RSV). And again he said, "Do not marvel that I said to you, 'You must be born anew'" (John 3:7, RSV). Publicans and sinners and scribes and Pharisees alike are the slaves of the same master, Satan, and none can be saved except they be born again. In another place Jesus added, "He who believes in the Son has eternal life; he who does not obey the Son shall not see life, but the wrath of God rests upon him" (John 3:36, RSV).

Jesus' description of the elder brother is a true-to-life photograph of the typical scribe or Pharisee. He is a man who wants to use God to exalt his own ego, to further his own purposes, and to prove his own importance. This committal becomes a compulsive force in his thinking. Unconsciously, it masters him. The result of this thinking shapes his concept of God. When such a person comes to maturity, his idea of God is pictured in his own image of himself. So it was then. The same is true today.

At this point the contrast begins. The younger son exploded in outbreaking rebellion. He knew what he wanted. His desires led him to gamble all in getting what God condemned. He loved sin. It promised satisfaction to his appetite and his ambitions. It lured him by its promises. Its fascinations hypnotized him. He had his fling. It was a binge that landed him where Jesus found the publicans and sinners. They knew themselves to be what they were. They had found in Jesus the answer to their need.

It was different with the elder son. He liked it at home. Not that he loved his father. Like the rest of us, he wanted to have his own way. He thought he was smart enough to manage his father and to get out of him what he wanted. He would capitalize on his father's reputation. He had sense enough to see that his father had wisdom. His father was a success. Knowing that about his father did not commit him to pleasing his father. He loved himself too much to be interested in pleasing anybody but himself. Pride born of self-conceit was his guiding star. Covetousness and envy were his motivating forces. Anger against those who challenged his thinking or purposes called him to battle. His self-appreciation magnified his conception of what he deserved. He did not break away from his father. It was too convenient and profitable to stay at home. In the depths of his heart, however, he was farther away than his younger brother.

Thus both sons had revolted against their father, the younger from parental control, the elder from parental love. Each wanted the same thing: to have his own way. Each, without realizing it, was attempting to play God, but in a different fashion. Each got his own way. Then developed the most striking difference in the picture. When each had reached his longest distance from his father, one of them came to himself and said, "Father, I have sinned . . . treat me as one of your hired servants." The other one railed on his father in criticism and whined in petulant anger, accusing his father of neglecting him.

In the beginning with each of the brothers, the younger and the elder, we are confronted with the soul that needs and lacks the new birth. It is one thing to have been created in the image of God. It is another thing, after sin has marred the image, corrupted the soul, and condemned the sinner, for that soul to become conscious of its sin and need and seek a saviour. Such a seeking soul enters into life's most blessed experience through receiving Jesus with abhorrence of sin, repentance for rebellion, and wholehearted surrender to Christ. The result is that life is utterly reborn through the grace of God in Christ Jesus.

It is difficult to make the crisis decision that marks the transition from self-righteousness to contrition for sin. In fact, it is more difficult for the self-righteous than for one whose experience of sin has either physically or socially or otherwise left his life a shambles of frustration and woe.

The elder brother did indeed have some virtues which deserve respect. Socially he had not brought reproach upon his father. His behavior marked him as a gentleman. He had resisted all temptation to physical dissipation. He had disciplined himself to respect himself and to respect other people according to the canons of social politeness. In many areas he could properly be regarded as a good son of his father.

He was industrious and thrifty. He despised slothfulness. He was the enemy of extravagance. He improved his opportunities to prosper that he might possess the essentials of life. It is a good thing for a man who has been born again to have some of the virtues of the elder son. He had found out some things about revealed religion that help a man to lead a more successful life. His tragedy grew out of the fact that he had neglected other things that were more important.

His conduct created no scandal. He was the enemy of moral laxity. He did not gamble. He condemned lawlessness. He required himself to abhor immorality. He was entitled to all the credit that was due him.

He was religious. He had sought to know the legal and sacramental requirements of his religion and to practice them. Thereby he thought he was gaining credits that would provide redemption from his faults and create a store of spiritual values for himself. In fact, he was seeking to build up a big spiritual bank account. Satan is not opposed to a man's being pious. He encourages the kind of piety the elder brother had. It is a piety that ignores the graciousness of God and flatters the self-esteem of the one who seeks it. It is a negative piety that boasts of the sins it has not committed and is blind to the sins that are destroying it. It is critical of the sins of others and eager to confess them while it exaggerates the importance of its own virtues.

The disposition to criticize others springs from the heart whose spiritual focus minimizes the good in others while it magnifies what it believes to be good in itself. The final result of this is that the heart grows cold and sympathy is dissipated. The springs of compassion dry up. Love dies, and scorn of others who are unfortunate flames into denunciation.

This elder brother had missed the high qualities in his father's life. The strongest points in his father's personality were, in his thinking, elements of weakness. He simply could not understand his father's patience, forbearance, and grief over the younger brother's absence from the home. His frozen soul regarded his father's compassion and generosity as evidences of the softness of old age. He had reached that dreadful day that comes to all who follow as he traveled when he despised the best but adored the second best. His heart had become so frozen by selfish conceit that he lacked understanding or compassion.

The return of his brother, unrebuked by his father, to such a gracious welcome raised in his mind a question. "What is the final difference between righteousness and sin?"

His brother was a notorious sinner; he himself was righteous. His brother deserved nothing except to be abused and upbraided; he deserved to be praised and honored. He was an utter stranger to what his brother had suffered because of his sin. He had no understanding of the depths of his brother's repentance and the woe of his contrition. Nor had he grasped in the least the total surrender his brother had made with an honest plea from an honest heart for mercy and pardon. These qualities of his brother that brought his father such joy and called forth the gracious welcome were nothing in the thought and appreciation of the elder brother.

This elder brother had some serious faults of which he was unconscious. Externally he looked good, but internally, while his goodness satisfied the demands of his fellow Pharisees, it failed to satisfy the demand of God, who looks not on the outward appearance but into the heart.

The elder brother was bewildered. Why weren't people sounding his praises? Why hadn't his father made a banquet to honor him? The servants were happy over the brother's return. Even the neighbors seemed elated. How could they be that way? He felt that he was friendless. Without realizing it, his religion had atrophied his capacity for joy.

Why had this happened? His thinking, his aspiring, his ambitions, his labors, and his goals were so centered on furthering his own chosen objectives for himself that he had been left cold, suspicious, cynical, hard, and unforgiving. He was so full of pride, conceit, hate, jealousy, faultfinding, sullenness, and self-pity that he had no capacity for happiness. He was one of those pious persons who have too much religion to keep them from enjoying the pleasures of sin and not enough of the right kind of religion to bring them the experience of joy in the Lord. This elder son lacked the discernment that would have enabled him to know that respectability sought as an end in itself has a tendency to make one loveless. The quest of a praiseworthy reputation in an effort to merit spiritual credit inescapably inflates self-esteem and robs one of life's most stable assets.

Perhaps it was fortunate that he was in the field when his brother returned. Had he been at home, he would doubtless have spoiled those blessed moments of his father's joy when he greeted the son who had died and was now alive again, who had been lost and now was found.

The elder son's behavior, because of his father's welcome to his repentant brother, proved that the father had two lost sons instead of one. His attitude that day showed that sin's deadly work in his own soul had wrought a ruin as total as that which had brought his brother to repentance in the far country.

There are multitudes, of whom the elder brother is a type, who cannot think of their disposition as being the evidence of sin. There is no law against such faults except the offended law of love. It is interesting to note that of the seven deadly sins of tradition, four are of the mind and spirit and three pertain to the flesh. It was the sins of the flesh—lust, gluttony, and sloth—that overwhelmed the prodigal. It was the sins of the spirit—pride, covetousness, envy, and anger—that took captive the elder brother. They are sins perhaps more deadly than the sins of the flesh. Those who are despoiled by the sins of the flesh finally come to a crisis. They feel an overwhelming sense of their sin. They know they need help. Unless they get help, they perish. It is much more difficult to bring the elder brothers to understand that the compelling urges of their lives which seem to be so desirable and pious are in actuality forces that drive them into destroying sins.

Basically, these sins of the spirit are born of a conceit that makes all desires seem righteous and good. In the end they are repelled by the sins of others and proud of their own. It is well to remember that while the younger son confessed that he had sinned, abhorred his iniquity, and prayed for pardoning mercy, the elder brother bragged to his God that he was superior to his brother. These sins of the spirit blind spiritual perception. They delude one into regarding good as evil and evil as good. They make one imagine nonexistent virtues. These facts add to the peril of the one who is the captive of the socially respectable sins of the spirit. On one thing we can depend: the wages of the sins of the spirit are the same as the wages of the sins of the flesh. In the end, the total is always death.

In our world today the extent of sin's damage is appalling. It is easy to see the results of the sins of the flesh. Doubtless, Satan himself becomes alarmed when he beholds the holocaust of destruction that he is creating among human beings because of the sins of the flesh. Such disasters can bring even sinning into disrepute. On the other hand, one can be quite certain that he finds great satisfaction in the dreadful disasters that the sins of the spirit are producing. They are the source of the covetousness, prejudice, discord, and hate that harry men and nations. They destroy peace of mind. They wither the souls of men, women, and children. They are the terrible fruits that embitter the lives of millions.

Here there is a warning for every man, sinner and saint alike. The self-righteous unbeliever has his dreadful share of the responsibility for the hurt of the world because of his sins of the spirit. It is also true that too many of us who know Christ as our Saviour have given hospitality in one fashion or another to the sins of the spirit and thereby have hurt the heart of God and caused our neighbors to stumble.

Modern Pharisees are numerous. Their perverted self-justification shows them to be the spiritual descendants of their kind who opposed Jesus. Outside the circle of church membership, they acclaim themselves as being superior to Christians. Inside the church, by their attitudes and actions they arrest the progress of the gospel. Theirs, now as then, is a soul-freezing, killing, deadly sin. They are self-deceived into believing that Jesus Christ cannot do for them as well as they are doing for themselves.

If one searches the gospel, he will find that Jesus did not have very much to say against the sins of the flesh. He was positively opposed to them. He knew how wicked and devastating they are. Their results are so self-evident that Jesus did not have to say anything. They openly carry their own condemnation.

The sins of the spirit are insidiously inscandalous. They easily deceive the public and those who are in their power into thinking either that they are harmless or, as a matter of fact, they are most desirable. It is difficult to awaken such sinners to a realization of their sin. It was because of this that Jesus denounced with blazing fury the sins of the spirit. Neither in history nor literature nor other places of religious revelation did the sins of the spirit as exhibited by the scribes and Pharisees receive such denunciation as Jesus heaped upon them. He knew them. He had been seeing them all of his life. They devoured widows' houses, and his mother was a widow. They proclaimed to all who would give attention that they were the most pious people in all the land, and he knew them for whited sepulchers. He called them hypocrites, a generation of vipers. Of them he declared that unless they repented, every one of them would perish. Jesus loved them as much as he did common sinners. But he knew that ultimately their peril was greater than the peril of the younger son. He knew that the devil is never so successful as when he deludes a man into thinking that he is righteous. Jesus wanted this parable, I am sure, to provoke many Christians to revise their concepts of the deadly sins.

One of the deadliest consequences of the sins of the spirit is that, finally, they bring one to believe that God should agree with him.

Such sinners aspire to possess the sanctuary of God. They did in Jesus' day. Ananias, Sapphira, Diotrophes, and a host of others wanted the high places in the church. Those whose experience has brought them an acquaintance with many churches know that not infrequently, self-opinionated, self-righteous church members, like the scribes and Pharisees, have gained the places of authority in the Lord's churches.

This poor, deluded other son of his father thought he had bought by his own labor and earnings the privileges of God. Hear him when he says to his father, "Lo, these many years I have served you, and I never disobeyed your command; yet you never gave me a kid, that I might make merry with my friends" (Luke 15:29, RSV). Sooner or later within the heart of all such self-righteous people there arises a similar complaint to God. It may not be voiced so that others hear. Sometimes it is. Probably most people at one time or another have questioned the fairness of God in the distribution of his gifts. Others seem to get what we never receive. Happy is the soul in whose thinking it is forever settled that one is saved by grace through faith, not because of anything we have done, but because of the gracious love of God that has saved us. Our salvation is not of works, else we would be lost forever.

Let it be remembered that all who enter into the feast must go in by the same door.

"Father, I have sinned." The story of the prodigal ended in a feast. It was a feast over which there was a shadow. That shadow was the pall of black despair that was over the heart of the elder brother. His sins doomed him because he would not recognize that they were sins. They damned him. They hurt his father's heart. They created overtones of sadness in the joyous feast which his brother's return brought. He lost fellowship by his self-exclusion. He sent himself forth into a dreadful night of discontent.

8

Few Say It

I have sinned . . .

LUKE 15:18

SUCH CONFESSION IS RARE; such penitence a virtue seldom met. Even in the Bible the words, "I have sinned," occur only thirteen times. And even these are not all genuine. Three times they were uttered by sinners who were insincere. They nullified their confession either by negative action or cancelled it by positive recantation. In three instances they were spoken in nonpersonal, literary situations where no immediate personal transgression is involved. Five times the sinner confessed when his guilt had trapped him. The proof of it could not be escaped. Confession could not be avoided. There was nothing left for the sinner to say. Such was the case of Aachan, Saul, and Judas Iscariot. In none of these instances was there a manifestation of repentance. They were profitless confessions.

Only twice in the Bible was the confession followed by action which indicated the sincerity of the confessor, his abhorrence of his sin, and his plea for pardon. These two confessions were from David and the younger son in the parable.

The plural form of this sentence occurs only fourteen times in the Bible. Eleven times the prophet of God was confessing the sins of the people to whom he ministered. These were not personal confessions. The prophet was heartbroken because of the hardness of heart of the people. In three instances a congregation's sinful disobedience had brought upon them dreadful calamity from which there was no escape until in desperation they turned to God with the cry, "We have sinned." So it was with the children of Israel when they were afflicted with the visitation of the fiery serpent. So it was after they had blasphemed in the worship of Aaron's golden calf. So it was when they refused to trust the leadership of God and enter the Land of Promise. In each of these cases those who were sincere received a great blessing, but they were a minority. The majority ignored their confession and perished.

From the third chapter of Genesis, when sin first made its tragic entrance into human experience, through the book of Revelation, the Bible a thousand times or more is proving beyond controversy that the soul that sins does surely die. From Adam's first meeting with God after his fall until the present hour men almost invariably blame others for their guilt. It may be said that God's supreme problem in bringing men and women to salvation is to get them to face squarely the fact of their sin and their inexcusable guilt. He wants them to see that they must repent or perish. Heaven's population eventually will be constituted only by those who, in the spirit of David and the younger son, abhorred their sin, confessed it, and prayed for pardon. The power of sin is proved in the lives of intelligent people who ignore the testimony of God and the experiences of others and continue to justify themselves in their guilt.

David and the younger son stand alone in the Bible as the

only ones whose confession of sin was honest. From the depths of their hearts they were sincere. Their confessions were followed by action that proved their spiritual integrity and brought the kiss of God's forgiveness.

King David and the younger son were honest because they used none of the techniques of rationalization which men so often employ when they think of or are forced to face the fact of their sin. They did not resort to Adam's alibi, which has been the pattern through which, in most instances, most men and women have sought to blame their sin on something or someone besides themselves. We need frequently to go back and read what happened there. It can explain so much of the problem that God has with us. We quote it as the Bible tells it:

So when the woman saw that the tree was good for food, and that it was a delight to the eyes, and that the tree was to be desired to make one wise, she took of its fruit and ate; and she also gave some to her husband, and he ate. . . . But the Lord God called to the man, and said to him, "Where are you?" And he said, "I heard the sound of thee in the garden, and I was afraid, because I was naked; and I hid myself." He said, "Who told you that you were naked? Have you eaten of the tree of which I commanded you not to eat?" The man said, "The woman whom thou gavest to be with me, she gave me fruit of the tree, and I ate" (Gen. 3:6,9–12, RSV).

Thus Adam began it, and we have followed his futile pattern of self-justification. He and Eve sinned. Their sin got into the spiritual bloodstream of the race. All of us are infected. It is something we got from our spiritual heredity, and therefore we are not responsible. If we are as foolish as Adam, we try to deny our own inescapable accountability for our own sins. Who of us has not dealt with his own sins as Adam sought to escape the consequences of his?

In doing this we have used all the excuses men have ever employed. Perhaps no one of us has ever used every one of them, but each of us certainly, first and last, has used many of them. As time goes on and man's knowledge of this and that is enlarged, he puts new clothes on the excuses, gives them a new style, or decorates them with a new shape. But the process is the same—the age-old process of rationalizing the blame for our guilt.

Modern science has almost made a cult of irresponsibility. If all actions are explainable in terms of their causes, there is no room for freedom or for responsibility. When Dennis the Menace takes a hammer and smashes a piano, then looks up and sees an amazed adult watching him, he exclaims, "I am a neurotic." The joke, of course, is that this is an adult excuse for an adult crime put into the mouth of a child. But is is really just as silly when adults say it. A man doesn't feel like working and loses his job. Or he gets drunk and beats his wife. Or his wife gets bored and beats the children. Or they both get so wound up in a mad round of time-pay-ment-purchased baubles and pleasures that they forget how to live. Or one of them shoots the other in a fit of rage. It's not their fault, we say. They are frustrated, or neurotic, or temporarily insane. And the courts give the murderer a one-year rest cure in a mental hospital.

More sins are blamed on the Oedipus complex than used to be blamed on the devil himself. Father image, mother im-age, maladjustment, ego, id, anima, repression, sublimation, compensation, and sex with capital letters—this is the lan-guage of modern man. We no longer think of a sense of guilt as an aid to wholesome repentance, the emetic of the soul. We call it instead an abnormality and do our best in every possible way to get rid of it. We do spiritual strip teases on psychoanalysts' couches; we mix tranquilizers with alcohol to achieve that perfect nirvana of relaxed enthusiasm; we think as positively as we can. We are neither responsible nor free. We have melted God's image down in a Freudian vat and have poured it into a grey flannel suit.

The children are no better. The last twenty-five years of educational practice have left them undomesticated. The high priests of pedagogy tell us that the child must be left free to express himself, that he must not be inhibited, that he must be helped to develop as fully as possible into that glorious but undefined anything which is himself. All things were made relative to the child. No goals outside the educational process itself were allowed. Everything done in school must be interesting and useful to the child right then and there, or it could not be done. The child is naturally good and is getting better and better all the time. All the teacher is supposed to do is stay out of the way and let the children learn as they will.

This utter nonsense should have been disproved for all time when Johnny first stuck a switch-blade into the belly of that foreign-looking boy who sat across the aisle. But it really wasn't Johnny's fault. Johnny's parents had had an argument the night before. Johnny's father had talked quite loudly, and his mother had cried. And besides, Johnny comes from a bad neighborhood. The people are crowded, and there is a lot of drinking, and all the boys over there are pretty rough, and there's no place to play except the streets, and his family can't afford a television, and Johnny is frustrated. It really isn't his fault.

It's never anybody's own fault. If I don't pass a course, the professor flunked me. If I get the promotion, I worked hard for it; if somebody beats me out, I didn't get the breaks. I am a failure because I didn't get to go to the right school, didn't know the right people, didn't inherit enough money, didn't marry the right wife. I am never, never, never a failure simply because I wasn't good enough.

Modern education, communication, social usage, and entertainment have created an almost impermeable steel wall around the mind and soul of man to protect him from the light of the truth of his real spiritual condition. Satan is employing all the arts and processes of popular culture to lead a man to call that which is good bad and that which is bad good. Above all, he tries to persuade the individual, the family, the community, and the nation that "You are right. Something or somebody else for whom you are not responsible is the cause of what you are that is undesirable." A lot of religious people have never faced the reality of their own personal sinfulness and have never cried out to God as did David and the younger son.

These two exercised the blessed gift that God has given all of us: the gift of self-criticism. The Bible presents to us no two characters more human and in many respects more attractive than these two but no two who had sinned more positively and outbreakingly than they did. Their experience testifies to the fact that regardless of how deep into sin a man may descend or how covered up with its abhorrent degradation a man may be there is still alive within him this priceless gift of God—the ability to criticize himself objectively. So long as sin has not narcoticized the soul, there is hope.

The sins of David and the younger son wounded them. Their pride, their self-esteem, and their conceit were dreadfully hurt by sin. Its consequences embarrassed them. Its former sweetness had turned into the bitterness of gall in their mouths. In the depths of that dreadful hour, each of them resolved to cry out to God and did so. Why the sudden and drastic change? The light of the power of self-criticism revealed to them the true picture of themselves in the mirror of God's knowledge and judgment of them. By the power of the Holy Spirit each saw himself as one whose sin had horribly afflicted him. Each knew that he and he alone was responsible for his sin. The light was too clear and the image too true to be palliated by any pharisaical excuse.

They not only saw themselves and what they were; their discovery of themselves created in them a better opinion of God. With their self-discovery they remembered the amazing graciousness of God.

From their experience every sinner can derive hope, if he is interested. God still sees in him that which constrains the divine compassion to desire his salvation. The Holy Spirit of God does and will illuminate the souls of sinners and bring them to hear the voice of God saying,

> Come now, let us reason together, says the Lord:
> though your sins are like scarlet,
>   they shall be as white as snow;
> though they are red like crimson,
>   they shall become like wool.
>
> ISAIAH 1:18, RSV

There was a day when the young Jewish statesman, Isaiah, with his heart broken, went into the temple to pray. That day the lamp of God shone into his soul and brought him a vision of the divine holiness and the consciousness of his own sin, and he cried,

"Woe is me! For I am lost; for I am a man of unclean lips, and I dwell in the midst of a people of unclean lips; for my eyes have seen the King, the Lord of hosts!"

Then flew one of the seraphim to me, having in his hand a burning coal which he had taken with tongs from the altar. And he touched my mouth, and said: "Behold, this has touched your lips; your guilt is taken away, and your sin forgiven" (Isa. 6:5–7, RSV).

Have not the majority of us transposed and thereby perverted this God-given gift of self-criticism into a habitual attitude wherein we confess our neighbor's sins?

That is what Adam did when he accused Eve of causing him to sin. She did have her responsibility in the matter, but she did not make up Adam's mind for him. Many husbands have said their wives did make a decision, and in a sense they have whenever the husband is willing for the wife to make up his mind for him. From that point of beginning in Eden, the habit of blaming someone else and of confessing the derelictions of another has become an ingrown element in human nature that is difficult to eradicate.

It was of this habit that Jesus was talking in his Sermon on the Mount when he said,

Judge not, that you be not judged. For with the judgment you pronounce you will be judged, and the measure you give will be the measure you get. Why do you see the speck that is in your brother's eye, but do not notice the log that is in your own eye? Or how can you say to your brother, "Let me take the speck out of your eye," when there is the log in your own eye? You hypocrite, first take the log out of your own eye, and then you will see clearly to take the speck out of your brother's eye (Matt. 7:1–5, RSV).

Long ago I heard a good man say, "Confessing my own sins is a full-time job. Since I realized that, I have not had time to confess the sins of my neighbor." It is easy for our people to confess the sins of the Russian Communists, but their sinfulness does not make us holy. As a nation we have every reason to be sitting in the sackcloth and ashes of humiliating contrition for our own sin.

Satan was surpassingly clever when he sold this fraud to men and women. Too many of them have bought the idea that they need not be disturbed about their own sins because other people are doing the same thing. This pattern of thinking quickly leads one to minimize his own faults and magnify the shortcomings of others. Likewise, he magnifies his small virtues and minimizes the graces of his neighbor. The pull of such thinking more and more distorts the focus of his vision and makes it increasingly difficult for him to exercise the gift of self-criticism. Eventually a man will condemn loudly the sins of others and ignore the very same sins in his own life. As he sees it, there are extenuating circumstances—but only for himself.

When Nathan told David the parable of the poor man who had only one little ewe lamb, whom he had loved and tended with diligent devotion, and of his rich neighbor who took away by force the only lamb of his poor neighbor, David was highly indignant. Immediately he tried him and condemned him to death for his crime. Then the long finger of God through Nathan pointed directly at David and accused, "Thou art the man." This tells us two important things about ourselves. One is that our own sins look outrageously ugly in somebody else. The other is that God sees and knows all about them. He is offended at them because of the hurt they do us and the damage they do to others. There is something in us that makes us dear to him. He wants to deliver us from their guilt and curse that we may enter into new life through his pardoning mercy.

All of this brings us to the fact that guilt must be faced or it remains to destroy!

In this parable Jesus meant to make it very plain that men and women can never have redemption from the guilt and curse of sin unless first they come face to face with the fact that they are sinners. Most of us are perfectly aware that many adults and even children are devoted to the discipline of high personal integrity. They never degenerate to the level of David's lust or the younger son's dishonor in the hog pasture. Neither had Saul of Tarsus. Nevertheless, of all those born of woman only Jesus has been sinless. "All have sinned and fall short of the glory of God" (Rom. 3:23, RSV).

Experience makes it very clear that even children, if the truth is clearly presented to them, come to the consciousness of sin. They realize they are lost and need a saviour. Young people and adults whose social reputations are above reproach become painfully aware of personal sin when they expose themselves to a clear picture of the purity and holiness of Jesus.

Jesus knew this. If ever there was a man in this world who could have been saved by the merit of his own moral, spiritual, and formal religious attainment, that man was Nicodemus. We should all remember that within the first two minutes of a brief conversation, three times Jesus told him, "Ye must be born again." Blinded by the pattern of his thinking, Nicodemus was utterly baffled by the statements of Jesus. Spontaneously he exclaimed, "How can these things be?" Satan had done his work well in the life of this holy but self-righteous moral man. And so he justified himself.

But the Word of God pursues us. In some way its light has fallen into our souls and has been captured and stored within the recesses of our unconscious and subconscious minds. God will not suffer any person to go the full journey of this life without confronting him as he confronted David through Nathan. Long may the devil deceive people. Frequently they give themselves credit for having more than they have. They are ingenious in their devices for their own self-justification. But no man who has any knowledge of the truth of God in his soul has ever failed to find himself in the crisis experience of standing alone in the light of the truth of the eternal God and knowing himself to be condemned. Certainly many people run from such a disturbing experience. God will not compel them to repent. Sooner or later he does bring them to face the facts about themselves. Their choice in such crises determines their destiny. Then, like David, they should cry out,

Have mercy on me, O God, according to thy steadfast love;
    according to thy abundant mercy blot out my transgressions.
Wash me thoroughly from my iniquity,
    and cleanse me from my sin!

For I know my transgressions,
    and my sin is ever before me.
Against thee, thee only, have I sinned,
    and done that which is evil in thy sight,
. . . .
Purge me with hyssop, and I shall be clean;
    wash me, and I shall be whiter than snow.
                              Psalm 51:1–4,7, RSV

If and when such a soul turns to God, God quickly forgives, saves, and satisfies. In no other way can one obtain forgiveness, for guilt must be faced before it can be destroyed. It must be confessed before God will pardon.

Everyone should remember that only he can face his guilt for himself; only he can abhor it, forsake it, confess it, and commit himself to God. Neither God nor society can do this for him. God will not permit a man's freedom of choice and the obligations of his personal responsibility to be forfeited by compelling a man against his will to abhor and confess his sin. Each possesses the awful responsibility of scorning or accepting Jesus Christ, of believing or disbelieving the warnings and promises of God's Word.

Parenthetically, we need to pause here to recognize that in the matters we have been considering we have the problem of both the sinner and the saint. By the sinner is meant the one

who has not come to an initial confrontation of God in Christ
and definitely accepted Christ to be his Saviour. When he
does abhor, confess, repent of his sins and commit himself to
Christ, he experiences the new birth and becomes the child
of God. As such, he is an infant saint. From that moment
Satan will seek to compromise him. He will continually be
exposed to temptation. Like the best saints of all the ages,
there will be times when he will yield. Upon one thing he
can count—it may be very soon or it may be later—he will
consciously stand again in the light of the truth of God. The
Holy Spirit will bring him to face his sin. He will know
that he has sinned. Unfortunately, many Christian saints have
become strongly wed to some of their sins. They do not easily
give them up. Their habit of self-justification persists. By
the techniques of rationalization, they develop a defense by
which they seek to build up for themselves release from the
accusations of the Spirit. If this attitude persists, the hand of
God's discipline will fall upon them. The author of the book
of Hebrews gives us this picture. In it he saw the experience
of every saint. Here he tells us how God deals with a Christian when he sins.

And have you forgotten the exhortation which addresses you as
sons?—
    "My son, do not regard lightly the discipline of the Lord,
      nor lose courage when you are punished by him.
    For the Lord disciplines him whom he loves,
      and chastises every son whom he receives."
It is for discipline that you have to endure. God is treating you
as sons; for what son is there whom his father does not discipline?
If you are left without discipline, in which all have participated,
then you are illegitimate children and not sons. Besides this, we
have had earthly fathers to discipline us and we respected them.
Shall we not much more be subject to the Father of spirits and
live? For they disciplined us for a short time at their pleasure,

but he disciplines us for our good, that we may share his holiness. For the moment all discipline seems painful rather than pleasant; later it yields the peaceful fruit of righteousness to those who have been trained by it (Heb. 12:5–11, RSV).

9

Our Second Prayer

Make me as one of thy hired servants.
LUKE 15:19

*"Treat me as one of your hired serv-
ants."*
LUKE 15:19, RSV

BATTER MY HEART . . .
JOHN DONNE

"Batter my heart." "Father, make me." This prayer is the
most sublime utterance in all the literature of man's spiritual
decisions. It is "our second prayer," the unselfish prayer, the
Christian prayer. It is part of the soliloquy that Jesus put into
the mouth of the younger son in the parable. It defines and
describes the triumph of God's quest for sinners. Jesus stated
it so clearly that only the blind or perverted can miss its
meaning.

But when he came to himself he said, "How many of my father's
hired servants have bread enough and to spare, but I perish here
with hunger! I will arise and go to my father, and I will say to
him, 'Father, I have sinned against heaven and before you; I am

no longer worthy to be called your son; treat me as one of your hired servants' " (Luke 15:17–19, RSV) .

This second prayer is the prayer of complete surrender. It is surrender without reservation, qualification, or equivocation. In the soul's first decision that brings the sinner to the new birth, the prayer, "Father, make me as one of thy hired servants," reveals the sense of awful need that motivates it. Those who pray it as Jesus meant for it to be prayed are those who have become desperate because of the consciousness of their own sinfulness. They know that they are ragged, hungry, and ashamed. Startled, they realize the disaster that their self-will has brought them. The love of God in Jesus Christ revealed by the Holy Spirit has set before them one lone star of hope. It is the light of the mercy of God that they have now come to see.

However, it fills the discoverer with shame to be thus confronted with God's compassion. While he has acted foolishly, he possesses areas of genuine human intelligence. He knows that, as men think and react, they despise him. He knows that God has every reason, from the human point of view, to loathe him. He has had his inheritance and has squandered it. It is dreadfully embarrassing to go trudging back home after having made such a fool of himself. He remembers that he once loathed his home. He had wanted only what his father could give that he could take to the far country. Equally he had wanted to get away from his father. Now he knows that having his own way was the worst thing that could have happened to him. For him it would have been infinitely better to have remained in his father's house as an underprivileged hired servant than to have come to what he knows himself to be.

Unfortunately for them, unbelieving sinners measure God by themselves. They imagine he thinks as they think, that his motives are like theirs, and that he deals with others as they would. Before they see themselves as the sinners they are, they foolishly think they are smarter than God. When the sun, moon, and stars of their self-esteem suddenly burn out and the earthquakes that follow the discovery of their true selves shock them with terror, they would be doomed forever unless the Holy Spirit in such moments brought them enough light from the love of God to enable them dimly to see the road to deliverance and home. The spiritual insight of too few of us has ever adequately enabled us to understand the height and depth, the length and breadth, and the wonder of what Jesus is revealing to us in the prodigal's great soliloquy.

Thirty years ago there lived in a good-sized city a man who was widely known in that community as its most godless citizen. He did not drink liquor or use tobacco; neither was he untrue to his wife or inconsiderate of his children. He was devoted to his friends.

But in his thinking, Christians were hypocrites, preachers were silly sissies, and money should be got by gambling, by cheating the law, and making its enforcement impossible. It was commonly believed that no criminal was convicted in court whom he wanted acquitted. He cherished some implacable hates. His vanity was enormous. He enjoyed getting what he wanted and preventing the people whom he disliked from receiving what they deserved. He thought he was having a lot of fun playing God. He enjoyed walking in the glamour of the notion that he was the town's big shot.

When he was about fifty years old, the long finger of the omnipotent and omniscient God touched him. The experience was mysteriously strange and bewildering. Suddenly he found himself unsettled in his thinking. In a little time he who had been as hard as nails, utterly cocksure, and strut-tingly aggressive, became unsure. He wondered if he were sick or if he were losing his mind. Was he on the verge of a nervous breakdown? He who had thought himself fearless became terrified. His sun had gone into eclipse. The skills upon which he had depended seemed to vanish. He was up against something he could not manage. What could he do? To whom should he go? The doctors and counselors whom he sought were not able to help. He found himself exactly where the prodigal made his amazing self-discovery in the far country.

When his soul had plummeted to the depths of the pit that he had dug for it, he began to remember his mother. She had died when he was in his late teens. In his way he had adored her memory, although from his early boyhood he had had no more respect for God than had the prodigal. His mother had been a Christian. Despite his resistance, she had planted many ideas of the gospel in his mind. Then, thirty years later, the Holy Spirit lifted up out of his unconscious mind a few verses of Scripture which his mother had made him memorize. He could not shake them off. He could clearly recognize the tones of her voice as she had pounded them into him, willy-nilly. In their truth he discovered what he had been—a disreputable, godless sinner. When he came to himself, he did the last thing he thought he would ever do. He sought the counsel of a preacher. The preacher had understanding enough to listen and rightly interpret what he heard. He knew the man's need and the gospel of Christ which could meet it. The godless one surrendered to Christ and was born again. His conversion created a sensation and set bells ringing in many souls.

I knew him well for the several years thereafter before he died. He never ceased to wonder at the amazing grace of God that saved him. Many times he said, "I am the total opposite of what I was before Christ saved me. I see differently, think differently. What I formerly loved, now I loathe. What I loathed, now I love."

In the fifty years that I have been a preacher I have personally known other conversions as extraordinary as this. Even so, they were the exceptional cases. The conversion of Saul of Tarsus was much more sensational than that of James and John and most of the other apostles. It is true that the conversion of Matthew, the chief publican with the best job in all Palestine, was a sensation. Still, though the extraordinary conversion is not so frequent, basically everything that happens in such conversions also occurs in all conversions that result in a spiritual new birth.

The sense of shock which one would experience while riding in a car traveling at seventy-five miles an hour that in two seconds reversed itself and traveled at an equal speed in the opposite direction, if he survived, would be overwhelming. But every day thousands of people, observing the rules of spiritual traffic, completely change directions with no sense of shock. They follow the established pattern, the general rules that characterize such changes. They are the normal, average boys, girls, and youths who gradually became acquainted with Christ under competent religious instruction. They learned to love him from their earliest remembered childhood. They have respected him in their parents, teachers, or ministers. Then they reach God's appointed season for the soul. The Holy Spirit confronts them with the fact that they are sinners. They need the Saviour. They accept him. He saves them.

The power that impels one to pray, "Father, make me," comes from the recognition of need that cannot be met otherwise. The degree and measure of its impact is determined by the facts of one's situation. With the young man in the parable, Saul of Tarsus, Augustine, Luther, and others, there was an overwhelming sense of guilt for the disaster which sin had brought. This guilt and contrition brought emotional stress, tension, reaction, and conscious force of commitment too great to exaggerate. There followed experiences of amazement and wonder that lasted until the last hours of their lives. Their introduction to the compassionate redemptive love of God suddenly lifted them out of the torments of the hell that was in their hearts to the mountaintops of celestial bliss.

In contrast, those who come to Christ while they are yet young, who have not had years of struggle, pain, and woe as the result of their sin, enter into satisfying experiences, but they do not feel the same wondering way about the amazing grace of God that has saved them. They are fortunate not to have suffered the wounds of sin which others have incurred. They lack the scars that remind others of their shame. In many ways they are more fortunate. At the same time, there are some lessons they will have to learn later. Their previous experiences have not taught them the folly of self-centeredness and conceit. In their spiritual development they are still largely living in the area of the first prayer: "Father, give me." This can become the dominating element in their prayer patterns and practices. Unconsciously, it can betray them into false expectations. They become susceptible to temptations that will pile up perils.

It is not too great a generalization to say that every Christian has to learn the hard way to give up praying, "Father, give me," and to pray confidently, "Father, treat me as one of your hired servants." Such a hired servant pleases not himself but his employer, seeks not his own will but his master's. Such a decision brings about a transfer of soul-sovereignty from the rule of self-will to the mastery of God's will.

Such a transfer initially occurs on life's greatest battlefield.

With Jacob it was in the all-night wrestling ordeal. Isaiah met it in the temple when he saw God high and lifted up. With Peter it was when he had the vision that led him to the house of Cornelius to preach to Gentiles. For Paul it was the Damascus road.

The one thing of which each person is supremely jealous by nature and inheritance is his self sovereignty, his right of self-determination. Whether one is converted early or late does not determine once for all this transfer of sovereignty. Its challenge poses a struggle for both sinner and saint. "Father, make me," continues to be a difficult prayer for most of us to pray when to do so we must honestly recognize that we prefer God's will to be done, even though it contradicts our dearest desires.

The difficulty increases because God will not overpower us and compel us to transfer our self-sovereignty to his mastery. This, perhaps, is best illustrated in the experience of Jacob. We know how heartily he wrestled, as one who loves the fray, with the angel in the first hour or hours of the contest. He wanted to win. We, like him, want to win on our own terms. When he could not win on his terms, he tried to trade. If he could not get all he wanted, he was eager to get what he could and still preserve the face of his pride. So the struggle lasted until the breaking of the day's dawn. He had exhausted himself in his contention with the eternal God. Frequently God mercifully lets us wear ourselves out. His patience is amazing in its compassionate forbearance.

At last, Jacob knew he was conquered. His spirit yielded when the wrestler sent from God touched his thigh and put it out of joint. Suddenly his resistance wilted. He had exhausted himself in seeking his own will. It was then that he discovered that God's will was far better than what he would have chosen. There are times when it is better to follow God blindly than to travel in the wrong direction. God's character is the guarantee that he will lead the trusting soul to better things.

One of the things that delays the time of full surrender, when we will pray, "Father, make me," is that we so intently want God to grant us his blessing on our terms. Few of us can understand that the way to God's best blessing is to ask for nothing for one's self, except to know and do his will.

Frequently in the last twenty years, as Christian people have heard me preach these ideas, deeply puzzled they have asked, "According to your idea, we cannot ask God for anything. Doesn't the Bible say, 'Ask and ye shall receive?' "

The answer to their question is that one is free to ask anything he chooses to ask. However, he is fortunate when he has learned what things are best.

Then for what should we pray? We have already seen the consequences of the prodigal's prayer. We know many people who get what they want and then prove themselves not competent to manage it after they get it. It would be a real revelation to us to find out what we miss because God does not answer some of our "Father, give me" prayers. His withholding of the gift is a blessing that saves us from great hurt.

Petulantly, adolescents nag their parents, "Father, Mother, give me an automobile." When denied, they frequently despise their parents. Others have tantrums when they are denied the use of the family car. Many are unhurt and living today because their prayer was denied. If one is to have God's favorable answer to his prayers, he will be wise to consider for what he should ask before he enters his plea.

This is a realization that depends much upon experience. One does not come to it suddenly. For what shall I pray? Most of us have understood that we have a problem at this point. Paul faced it and gave us a good insight when he wrote, "Likewise the Spirit helps us in our weakness; for we do not know how to pray as we ought, but the Spirit himself intercedes for us with sighs too deep for words. And he who searches the hearts of men knows what is the mind of the Spirit, because the Spirit intercedes for the saints according to the will of God" (Rom. 8:26–27, RSV).

Many of us when we were children eventually discovered that our fathers and mothers could choose better for us than we could choose for ourselves. After we have assumed life's full responsibilities, we continue to learn that the judgment of others in many things is superior to our own. The longer most of us live, the more we know that we do not have sense enough to commit ourselves to doubtful requests. However, we do have a God whom we can trust.

Therefore, we are wise to limit our asking of God to the areas that are not influenced by self-interest. It is highly profitable to pray for such things as these:

> *For a Thankful Heart;*
> *For a Soul that Abhors Evil;*
> *For Grace to Love God Supremely;*
> *For Hunger and Thirst After Righteousness;*
> *For Purity of Heart and Motive;*
> *For God's Blessings to Be on the Troubled,*
> *the Bewildered, the Tired, the Sick,*
> *the Tempted, and Sinful, to Turn Their*
> *Hearts unto Him in Trusting Faith.*

We should ask God for faith and for understanding of the Word of God and the needs of those whom we might serve.

We should ask for God's guidance through all the circumstances of life.

We should ask God to warn us of the approach of temptation and help to deliver us from it to his glory.

We should ask him for his blessing to be upon our friends

and loved ones, upon strangers and enemies, and upon our work, that we may do it according to his will.

By all means, we should pray for ministers, missionaries, teachers, those who rule over us, and those who influence our neighbors and ourselves.

There are a thousand wonderful things for which to pray, not one of which is designed to add a dime to our purses or the least lift to our egos or to enhance our own reputations.

The effective and irresistible prayer is a selfless prayer. The only self-concerned prayer we can pray is for God to help us find the things that are good and right for us as we serve him and try to do his will.

Those who have prayed like this have discovered that they have found the key to God's storehouse. They have learned that God never fails to answer selfless prayers. He answers more wonderfully than all expectation prayers mastered by a desire that God manage the matter as his wisdom directs. Once one has come to that point in his soul, he has his hand in his Heavenly Father's hand.

Once he has broken through to such a personal understanding of God, his fears are gone. He knows that he lives in a world of trouble. His Bible has told him plainly: "Many are the afflictions of the righteous; but the Lord delivers him out of them all" (Psalm 34:19, RSV).

He knows that, beginning with Abel, all of God's saints have suffered. Their sufferings fall into many categories. Many have endured persecution for righteousness' sake. Others have experienced innumerable personal trials. The afflictions of some are publicly known, while those of others are known only to themselves. Can one find in the Bible a single great servant of God who did not have to endure grievous trials of some description? Christian history is filled with stories of the thousands who suffered arrest, false charges, harsh penalties and, in many instances, martyrdom for their faithfulness to their God.

Some afflictions do not come from persecution. Some Christians have endured the trials of intense pain from physical illness that have lasted through intermittent seasons or a long period of years. Disasters of various kinds overtook them, and tragedies befell them. Still others have innocently suffered great embarrassment. Their hearts were broken through no fault of their own but by reason of hurt which they received from the sins of others. For the Christian, suffering is no respecter of persons or social situation. Inexplicable bereavements and bewildering losses come to all.

The Scriptures and the experience of the saints of the centuries prove beyond all doubt that while God does not spare his children suffering, he does sustain them with his grace. They come to know what Paul learned and was inspired to write:

What then shall we say to this? If God is for us, who is against us? He who did not spare his own Son but gave him up for us all, will he not also give us all things with him? Who shall bring any charge against God's elect? It is God who justifies; who is to condemn? Is it Christ Jesus, who died, yes, who was raised from the dead, who is at the right hand of God, who indeed intercedes for us? Who shall separate us from the love of Christ? Shall tribulation, or distress, or persecution, or famine, or nakedness, or peril, or sword? As it is written,
     "For thy sake we are being killed all the day long;
       we are regarded as sheep to be slaughtered."
No, in all these things we are more than conquerors through him who loved us (Rom. 8:31–37, RSV) .

When such experiences befall faithfully trusting hearts, God invariably helps. Paul and Silas, after being falsely ac-

cused by the covetous enemies of God, were scourged un-
lawfully, thrust in the Philippian dungeon, and fastened by
their feet in the stocks. Under such circumstances those who
have not learned that nothing can separate us from the love
of Christ will be overwhelmed. Those who have learned it
have a song for such midnights. Luke tells us, "But about
midnight Paul and Silas were praying and singing hymns to
God, and the prisoners were listening to them" (Acts 16:25,
RSV). One wonders what their song might have been. We
know that their hymnbook was the Psalms. Legend has it
that their hymn was Psalm 46. It might well have been.

> God is our refuge and strength,
>   a very present help in trouble.
> Therefore we will not fear though the earth should change,
>   though the mountains shake in the heart of the sea;
> though its waters roar and foam,
>   though the mountains tremble with its tumult.
>
> There is a river whose streams make glad the city of **God**,
>   the holy habitation of the Most High.
> God is in the midst of her, she shall not be moved;
>   God will help her right early.
> The nations rage, the kingdoms totter;
>   he utters his voice, the earth melts.
> The Lord of hosts is with us;
>   the God of Jacob is our refuge.
>
>   PSALM 46:1–7, RSV

The legend says that all the time God had been listening
to their song with the others. When they reached that last
line, he reached down and with his all-powerful hand got
hold of the foundation rock that was deep down under that
jail and began to shake it with exactly the right force and direction of movement. By the vibration that followed all of the

locks were shaken loose and the stocks fell off the prisoners' feet.

Looking back along the trails of memory through fifty years spent in the ministry, I feel sure beyond question that the happiest people whom I have ever known were Christians who had suffered much. It is ever so with those whose prayers is, "Father, make me."

There are those who have experienced failure in their ventures in self-management. They have known the travail of a contrite heart. Pain over the guilt of sin brought them to abhor it and to confess it. Out of this repentance came a decision that changed everything. In the terms that Jesus so perfectly described, there was a day when they also said, "I will arise and go to my father, and I will say unto him . . ." They yielded to God the management of their lives. His pardon and grace flooded their souls with blessings.

Of course, Satan came back to tempt them again and again. At times they slipped into the habit of their "Father, give me" days. By a pious rationalization they sought to gild their selfish desires with holy aims or to excuse sin with self-righteous justification. God was patient with them. The Holy Spirit called them to repentance. When they kept on arguing, chastisement began. The Lord let them suffer the consequences of their sins as much as was necessary. Finally, corrective discipline was effective.

Unfailingly, however, God always sustains the afflictions of those whose hearts are stayed on him. He uses their trials to build a golden stairway up which their hearts can journey to the inner sanctuary of his love.

Experience finally teaches those who have learned the meaning of our second prayer that it is the only prayer to pray. Through it they have learned that their God "is able to do far more abundantly than all that we ask or think" (Eph.

3:20, RSV). They have found and experienced the reality
of the blessed God "who is able to keep you from falling and
to present you without blemish before the presence of his
glory with rejoicing, to the only God, our Savior through
Jesus Christ our Lord, be glory, majesty, dominion, and authority, before all time and now and for ever. Amen" (Jude
24–25, RSV).

10

The Journey Home

"I will arise and go to my father."
LUKE 15:18, RSV

And he arose and came to his father.
LUKE 15:20, RSV

CONSIDERING HIS TOTAL CONDITION, how did this younger son develop the motivation necessary to make the decision to go home and to carry it into effect? This is an important question. We will miss much if we do not get the right answer for it. Surely Jesus wanted people to understand what is involved in this question. The answer is to be found in what happened to him "when he came to himself."

The thing that made him "wise to himself" was the fact that he who had been so self-sufficient, who could not be wrong and could not fail, suddenly found himself to be ragged, dirty, hungry, shelterless, and bedless. Now that the worst had happened, the beautiful fantasies of his conceited, wishful thinking evaporated. He was aware of the stark realism into which he had foolishly stumbled. He was quickly able to understand what had happened. He knew that he was responsible for what had occurred. It is encouraging to find

that he didn't alibi or blame someone else. Fortunately, he
was honest enough and wise enough to face the facts as they
were. Can any other explanation reasonably account for the
decisions and actions that followed?

Once he reached this point, he thought clearly and straight.
The Holy Spirit must have led his imagination to recall the
picture of the meals that were served to his father's hired servants in the days of his childhood and youth. They were solid
and adequate. They lacked the finer delicacies of his father's
table, but they satisfied hunger and gave strength for work.
Instantly the contrast shocked him—the diet of his father's
servants and his, which was to share in the food of the hogs.
There was famine in the land. Many of the banquets which
sin provides for a season will inevitably have a last night of
revelry which will end in a new day of want. Then the wastrel will find himself helpless to provide further for himself.
In this picture Jesus is painting the certain last days of spiritually starving sinners.

This startling recognition of the superior situation of his
father's servants to his situation quickly changed the prodigal's perspective. How long it took him to come to a decision
would be pure speculation. There are some who persist in
the agony of the deep consciousness of sin's guilt for a long
time. They finally starve and die in their sin. Others resist for
days or months and then decide to change their course. There
are some who do not tarry long; once their real condition is
clear, they quickly decide and follow through. The time fac-
tor is important, but not so important as the fact that for the
first time since at least months before he left his father's
house the young man's thoughts were right according to the
relevant facts.

His changed thinking led him to remember his father. Until this happened, he had refused, as much as he could, to

think about him. When he had thought of his father, he did not admire the image that he saw. This happened because he was looking at his father through the distorted lights of his prejudice, self-centered conceit, and foolish delusions. Now that these were gone, in imagination he beheld his father's face as he had seen it before the clouds of vanity had obscured the clarity of his perception.

Jesus is here writing an important chapter in the spiritual biography of every sinner. It is one that too few of us have bothered to find and read. It is one that is true to the life experience of each one who has wandered far away from God, then in the depths of need comes to himself and makes the same decision.

In the new look which he gave to his image of his father's countenance, the prodigal beheld a quality of compassion, selfless love, and eagerness to help those who are in need that had always characterized his father. Hitherto he had seen these as traits of weakness. Now he saw in them qualities that led him to hope. He would be a thousand times better off as a hired servant in his father's house than where he was.

Many have criticized his motive. Thirty years ago I heard an intelligent, scholarly lawyer teach a Sunday school class when this parable was the subject of the lesson. He severely criticized the motivation of the younger son's return home. He did a thorough job of berating him. His tone and attitude bespoke something of the hostility of the Pharisees and scribes toward the publicans and sinners.

More than twenty years ago I was the pastor of a church in which, without doubt in my mind, the best Christian and the most effective Christian leader in that city was a man who twenty-five years before had been the town's biggest sinner. He had come to himself and in the same spirit had gone forth with the same confession to meet his God. God instantly forgave him and blessed him, but the people did not. Some members of his own church and good Christian people in other churches in the community never forgave him for his early sins.

Beyond any doubt, the quality of the prodigal's confession, "Father, I have sinned against heaven and before you; I am no longer worthy to be called your son; treat me as one of your hired servants" reveals his new opinion of himself. The miracle of his change is working. The springs of his motivation are rapidly purified. His resolution is enriched. These decisions stimulate him. He must get back home. He must get back to his father. The important thing is to right himself with his father. His need and desire for food becomes secondary to the more important necessity of reconciliation with his father.

His awakening brought a great change. Quickly he made a complete decision. This far country to which he had gone so gaily was a long way from his father's home. I met one like him more than thirty years ago. He had walked forward from the rear of the church to give me his hand in the prodigal's confession and surrender to Christ. The weather was bitterly cold outside. The temperature inside was barely high enough for comfort. But this man's hand was dripping with perspiration. Later he told me about it. The agony of his soul's struggle was such that the hundred feet that he walked to give me his hand was one of the longest journeys he ever traveled. The man who told me this was a stable, honest man. After long years of refusing Christ, he came to himself, saw himself as he was, made the decision the prodigal made, and then traveled the long road that was the proof of his sincerity.

So it was with the younger son when he arose and went to his father. Something within him drove him to that journey. Every step was long and hard. He was ashamed. His thoughts

troubled him. Twenty years ago, just after we had finished
our noonday meal on Sunday, the doorbell rang. A young
married man, about thirty years old, whose wife belonged to
our church, was there. He was not a Christian but normally a
respectably decent fellow. By his face I saw that he was troubled. He was emotionally taut. I invited him in and seated
him in a deep armchair. I gently asked him what I could do
for him. His emotional disturbance rendered him temporarily speechless. I watched him closely and told him that a lot
of people had come to see me in the years past. They had
told me many things that embarrassed them in the telling,
but that in most instances they had found help in it. I told
him to take his time and that I wanted to help in whatever
way I could. His face grew more grim, and I knew that unless
he got himself in hand, there would soon be an emotional con-
vulsion. In not more than a minute after he was seated, he
pitched headlong forward out of that chair full length on the
rug and began to roll as he writhed in agony. I got hold of
one of his hands, exerted a gentle but steadily firm pressure
toward lifting him up, and got him back in the chair. By that
time he had broken into convulsive weeping. After sufficient
time for the pressure to reduce itself, his tension gradually
abated. With deepest shame, he told me what happened. He
had wronged the one whom he loved most. His shame and
grief made a terrible picture, but they were the travail out of
which was born a new man and a new husband for the wife
whom he had wronged.

As the younger son traveled as fast as his strength could
carry him on the way home, again and again he had to face
the humiliation of his stupidity. His previous folly had become unbelievable to him. How could he have been so foolish?

Three things disturbed him; three things trouble many

such prodigals. First, there was the embarrassment of facing the folks who had known him in his youth and were acquainted with his proudly ambitious exit from their community. What people think and say exerts a powerful force in many of life's situations. Nowhere is this more true than in the areas of moral and social status. This is especially so when one has plummeted from the heights of exceptional privilege to the depths of dishonoring want. Chief among those whom he dreaded to meet was his elder brother. There had never been any love lost between them. His brother had always been severely critical of him. It was obvious that he believed that his kid brother lacked both sense and character. Through his child's instinct he had sensed the hypocrisy of his self-righteous elder brother. One of his reasons for leaving home had been that he might escape association with him. It was clear to him that the elder brother stayed at home, not because he loved his father, but because he loved the special privileges and opportunities that he could enjoy unearned as the son of his father in the home community. To face that brother as he had become was a terrible thought to contemplate.

The second center from which troubled thoughts arose to harry his homeward journey was his realization that he had hurt his father. It was clear to him then that he had scorned his father's love. Sin's delusions had created irrepressible conflict between them. It was all his fault.

Jesus was aware at this point of the conflict that is engendered in adolescent minds against parents. People were no different basically in those days from what they are now. Neither has our increased knowledge significantly modified our own inner reaction. It is not unusual for girls in their teens to become wiser than their mothers. In most instances boys from sixteen to eighteen are smarter than their fathers.

Forty years in the pastorate brought me frequently into immediate contact with these situations between daughters and mothers and sons and fathers. It happens in the best homes and families. When children rapidly grow to the physical stature, strength, and capabilities of adults, when they have acquired a little sophomoric learning about a lot of things, they immediately decide they have the judgment to run their own lives. But they do not. They are not qualified to think as their parents think. Therefore, they see things differently. Deep within themselves they are aware of their inferiority to their elders in these respects. They seek to compensate for their deficiencies by aggressive self-assertion. They are driven to revolt against those older than themselves. Their principal targets are their parents. What an opportunity these facts create for Satan to produce a tragedy! Wise is the parent who remembers how she or he thought and acted at that younger age. Long ago someone said that the later teen-age youth is continually amazed at the ignorance of his parents. After they are twenty-one, they are surprised at how much Father and Mother have learned in recent years. When they are forty, they are certain that if they lived a thousand years they would never know as much as their parents.

The road over which this returning prodigal journeyed was one that sons and daughters frequently travel at some time in life when they are impelled to confess and pray for forgiveness to parents whom they have hurt. It can prove to be the most profitable thing they ever did. Pre-eminently this is true in the soul's return to God.

The third and most devasting thought that troubled him on the trek home was the utter humiliation he suffered because he had lost face with himself. The pangs of the torturing pain which follow a basic loss of self-respect are agonizing. Not many have sufficient courage to face them. In every possible way they seek to escape. Although God forgives, they cannot forgive themselves. There are thousands of solitary drunkards who drink themselves into unconsciousness every night in an effort to buy a few hours' escape from the anguish they suffer because they have lost their self-respect. Those who do not go to such desperate means hide from themselves in many and manifold rationalizations.

When his self-respect is wounded, a person is in crisis. Such a horrid perception of one's sinful stupidity brings him to the decision point. Heaven or hell for both time and eternity— this is the choice. Many there are who run from it, who find the glaring light of truth, the razor's edge of choice, too painful and sharp. They flee, not knowing that even this is a choice. The most pathetic of them wind up on the skid rows of large cities, in the back lots behind railroad yards, under bridges, and in jails. But the majority of them do not become social outcasts. They cultivate blind spots; they patch up the holes in their souls with business preoccupations and temporal troubles. They refuse to admit that there is anything wrong. They are keeping their problems in the outer office, hoping that eventually they will go away. They will not ask any overwhelming questions because they are afraid of being overwhelmed by the answer. But they do not know that not asking will also overwhelm them; that the end thereof is also death.

Everyone has sinned. Blessed are those who can admit it, even though the admission be painful. Sin is intensely personal. It originates in one's deepest and most private nature. Its results assault him and send him into revolt against God and into conflict with his fellow men. When a man realizes that he has sinned and what sin is, inevitably he is terrified. The truth about sin is always more horrible than the sinner could possibly have imagined. But it is out of this travail, out of this death of the old life of blindness and self-deception that the new life is born. This, in some dim measure, the prodigal had come to see. Fogs of uncertainty dimmed his vision about many things. But one thing he knew: He did not want to die the rotten death of a starved hog-herder. He had lost all faith in himself. But his new-grasped faith in his father was yet to be proved. One compulsive urge possessed him—he must go home.

To get home, he had to travel the same distance back to his father that he had traveled away from him. He had to come all the way back from the far country. His resources for the journey were so obviously inadequate that merely beginning it was a miracle of faith. Blessedly, this is all that is necessary. The faith that enables him to start is all that anyone has, or needs, for the journey back to a forsaken and forgotten God. If the prodigal had been forced to depend only on his own resources, he would never have made it. In our own strength we can never make it into the presence of God. Driven by a sense of supreme need, we take only the first step of an emerging faith.

It is indeed a long way home. Whether geographically, socially, financially, or spiritually, it is always a long way back from the far country of wrong, or shame, or sin. Many people are so frightened by the total distance that they never begin. They don't come to Christ because they are afraid they can't hold out. They try instead to wait until they have resources that can guarantee the whole journey. They want to be sure they won't backslide or falter at all before they start.

They will never make it. They are trying to deny life itself. One cannot breathe now enough oxygen for next week or eat in one meal enough food for a month. Just so, one cannot store up the resources essential to victorious Christian living before he takes the first step of the journey with Christ, the journey to God. God has the resources we need. Whenever a person dares to take that first step, determined by God's grace to go all the way, God always keeps him going. God always gives the step-by-step resources that the traveler needs.

The younger son's faith, which made him get up and start out, was the faith of a beginner. It pointed in the direction of his father's house—in the direction of a new life in God. Such faith is never disappointed. Invariably it is rewarded. The prodigal may have been greatly confused. But he did have his direction straight, and he was driven by the force of a purpose that God forever honors. The journey would be filled with struggle, hardship, and trial. Remorse, penitence, and shame would storm, darkening the sky and miring the road. But the prodigal was sustained by the hope that his father would be kind—that his father would give him the servant's place. Gradually his thoughts took form. The clouds slowly lifted and the fog disappeared.

His mind cleared about many things. For one thing, he was not cheating himself any more. He had swindled himself out of a glorious inheritance because he had believed in the lying snares of Satan. Like so many people, he had spent his fortune on glitter; he had paid out good cash to buy only gold mines in the skies of tomorrow. It is a great day for any man when he stops swindling himself.

He also had the right attitude toward his father. He had considered his father an old fool; his vanity had gilded his adolescent thinking and made it look like wisdom. He was sure he was the most brilliant young genius ever. But when the scales of delusion fell from his eyes, he saw himself and his father in the light of reality. He was the fool. His father had been wise. But this revelation no longer discouraged him. Rather, it gave him strength. To be with his father, to have the benefit of his father's wisdom, the security of his father's authority, the blessing of his father's approval—this was what he wanted. The one thing he wanted supremely was to square himself with his father.

All that he had to offer was an honest confession. But this confession was clothed in a newly found sincerity and backed up by an honest humility. He was the penitent, anxious only for life with his father, even on the lowest and meanest of terms.

He had desired independence and self-glorification. Now he desired dependence and authority. The position of hired servant in his father's household had become a thing far more precious than all the independence he had previously desired. His father would be responsible for him and would tell him what to do. Whatever his father told him to do would be the best thing to be done. Its results would be happily satisfying. As his father's hired servant, he could not fail to be a success. The prodigal, in returning to his father, was the archetype of all those who realize the love of God, the character of God, and the purpose and promise of God and then commit themselves to obedient service under God's absolute authority and will.

The frustrations and failures that had destroyed the prodigal's selfish dreams had shocked him into a tormenting fear. It is a fear that clutches the souls of many men. They are aware of what they want, but they do not know how to possess it. Jesus knew this. Upon the canvas of this picture he makes it so clear that none need misunderstand nor forget: It is that the only place of real security for a human soul is to be employed as a servant in his Father's house. In the latter stages of his journey home surely this must have been the thought that most possessed this penitent's mind. His real goal was security from

His own conceits, folly, and weakness;
Those who had been likeminded with himself;
The forces that had brought him disaster;
The perversions that had deceived him;
The false ideas that had corrupted him;
The failure, want, and woe that wasted him.
As a hired servant in his father's house,
He would have real security.

11

The Unexpected Welcome

> *And he arose and came to his father. But while he was yet at a distance, his father saw him and had compassion, and ran and embraced him and kissed him. And the son said to him, "Father, I have sinned against heaven and before you; I am no longer worthy to be called your son."*
> LUKE 15:20–21, RSV

IT COULD HAVE BEEN that the younger son slept out under the open sky the last night of his journey back to his father. By that time his mind had cleared about many things. Then he was only a few hours away from his destination. Already he was in an area which he knew from his childhood.

Since that day in the hog pen when he awakened to full awareness of his dreadful plight, much had happened to him. He now felt a sense of relief and release from the pressures of the driving power of sin. His emotions were more stable. Through the disaster he had gained a new maturity. Right thinking had opened new vistas of perception and understanding. On this last night away from home his thoughts were much occupied with his childhood.

117

This younger son must have had a happy childhood. His father had been the center of much of its richest delight. He had been eager to grow up to be a man like his father. His father saw in him the unfolding fulfilment of his soul's highest desire. His father understood him then, and he totally trusted, admired, and respected his father. Theirs was a normal relationship.

The growing independence that comes to the child when he is about ten years old is important. He is capable of doing more for himself. By the time he is twelve he believes he is competent to do more than he is actually able. He wants to impress the adults in the orbit of his life with his increased powers. When he has become an adolescent at fifteen, in order to prop up his self-esteem, he unwittingly imagines that he is much wiser and greater than he is. This brings him into collision with adult thinking. Adults do not accept him at his estimate of himself. By aggressiveness he tries to sustain the picture he has projected of himself. Then from sixteen to twenty there is apt to develop a great gulf between himself and the adults nearest to him. Communication is hampered or interrupted between them. Too often each misunderstands the other too much. Each becomes afraid of the other, though perhaps without being conscious of the fear. On the surface, in most instances, the relationship does not appear to have been greatly disturbed. But, as a matter of fact, even the boy who adored his father at the age of nine, at the age of fifteen often finds it difficult to stand his father's company. The two have become somewhat allergic to each other.

These facts are apparent everywhere in the mid-twentieth century. While they were less apparent generally in other generations before, the conflicts were no less real. The struggle will come to its conclusion when the father recognizes that the son has grown up to be a man and accepts him as such in the many respects in which he has acquired that status and when the son awakens to the fact that much, too much, of his thinking about his father is wrong.

Under these circumstances it could very easily have been that on this last night of his absence from home the younger son remembered clearly his childhood and the father whom he knew then. Memory can furnish a heaven of happiness or a hell of horror.

The prodigal had traveled through the hell of horror. He had been stridently scourged by memory from the time of his awakening in the far country until he was far on the road back home. At last some measure of release had been granted him, and clear thinking had turned his feet into the road that led him to his father.

He awakened refreshed at the coming of the day. Before that morning, sleep had not restored the strength of previous days. In spite of what the years had brought to him and his father, that morning he knew that deep down inside of his "I" that was enclosed by his "me" there was that same little boy yet alive in spite of all that had happened. He knew that his father was the same great person whom he had loved and adored. He had lost his vanity, ambition, self-conceit, and sin. They had become indescribably foolish to him. They had captured him, deceived him, and possessed him. Now he knew them to be what they were. In his childhood he had learned that God hated sin. From the Scriptures he had memorized the promise,

> Come now, let us reason together, says the Lord:
> though your sins are like scarlet,
>   they shall be as white as snow;
> though they are red like crimson,
>   they shall become like wool.
>
> ISAIAH 1:18, RSV

From the Bible study of his childhood he also remembered:

> But he was wounded for our transgressions,
>   he was bruised for our iniquities;
> upon him was the chastisement that made us whole,
>   and with his stripes we are healed.
> All we like sheep have gone astray;
>   we have turned every one to his own way;
> and the Lord has laid on him
>   the iniquity of us all.
>
> ISAIAH 53:5–6, RSV

He had been taught that these were the words of God—blessed promises that were fulfilled to believing, trusting hearts.

We must not forget that this penitent soul typified the publicans and sinners. They were Jews who had been instructed in their religion. Though they were in revolt against the doctrines and religious attitudes of the scribes and Pharisees, they were acquainted with the Word of God. Jesus knew this. After his awakening, it could hardly have been possible that the younger son would have failed to hear sounding out of the record of memory:

> Ho, every one who thirsts,
>   come to the waters;
> and he who has no money,
>   come, buy and eat!
> Come, buy wine and milk
>   without money and without price.
> Why do you spend your money for that which is not bread,
>   and your labor for that which does not satisfy?
> Hearken diligently to me, and eat what is good,
>   and delight yourselves in fatness.
>
> ISAIAH 55:1–2, RSV

Therefore, when the prodigal awakened to the new morning of the day that was to take him to his father's house, the Holy Spirit of God had conditioned his mind and soul for the experiences that awaited him. What happened to him has occurred also in the experience of all the other prodigals since his day who, like he, came to the hour when they cried unto God: "I have sinned against thee. Oh, God, have mercy upon me!" The Spirit of God, using his Word, guided and sustained the quest of their penitent hearts. It was God who had called the prodigal to go back home. He never calls one to make a journey that he can successfully travel alone. He has committed himself to accompany the penitent pilgrim who hears his call,

> Seek the Lord while he may be found,
>   call upon him while he is near;
> let the wicked forsake his way,
>   and the unrighteous man his thoughts;
> let him return to the Lord, that he may have mercy on him,
>   and to our God, for he will abundantly pardon.
>   ISAIAH 55:6–7, RSV

With this providential preparation for his final progress, the prodigal hastened on. He knew this road. With mounting excitement he remembered that when he got around the next turn, he could see his father's house. Soon he saw it. He stood still to drink in the enchanting vision it gave him. It was more beautiful than he had remembered it to be. Previously he had compared it with the rumored dream cities of the far country. His prejudice had perverted his vision. The old home had suffered in comparison with the tinsel glitter of the life he thought he would find in another land.

His soul became intoxicated with that first view. Then he became aware that a man had left the house and was running to meet him. "Who can it be, and why is he running?" he wondered. He did not remember any servant who ran like this one, and he knew it was not his elder brother—he rarely ever ran. The one who ran was like his father. He remembered his father's running when they played games together when he was a boy. It could not be his father, however, because his father was too old to run like that. Thus he speculated until the father was near enough to recognize beyond all doubt. He was astounded that his father ran so fast. But he was more amazed at the radiance of his father's countenance.

Surprise froze him in his tracks. Before he could think further, his father had reached him.

Their emotions were too deep for any greeting but silence at first.

Action pantomimed the message each gave: The father's face signaled compassion and unutterable joy. The son's countenance expressed speechless surprise. The father fell on the son's neck and kissed him.

Then the son shivered from the consciousness of his sense of his sins' guilt. How could he have so misunderstood such a father!

He had wondered how he could ever get the courage to face his father. The surprise of his father's joy over his return triggered his tongue, and the words burst forth from the depths of his soul, "Father, I have sinned against heaven and before you; I am no longer worthy to be called your son" (Luke 15:21, RSV).

To the prodigal's astonishment, the father interrupted his confession and stayed him before he could utter his prayer for forgiveness. His sin was not mentioned. The father knew all about it; but, better still, the father knew that the son had come home of his own choice. He knew that the one whom he loved and had lost for a while was found. He rejoiced that the son, who had been as one dead to him, was now alive and was to be so forevermore. He instantly ordered preparations to be made for a banquet to be served that would match, in the richness of its provision, the joy of his heart that his son had come home.

Jesus meant this to be a picture of God and ourselves. Here he is telling us the story of our self-willed breaking away from himself into adventures far from God. In it he has shown us the inescapable consequences of sin. From his own struggles with temptation, Jesus had learned how persuasive Satan is. He understood human nature. He knew what people thought and how they thought. He did not exaggerate sin because he knew exactly what it is, and what it is is too deadly to be exaggerated. No one has ever painted this picture as clearly as Jesus paints it in this parable. Its portrayal of God's attitude toward sinners and the sinner's attitude toward God is unsurpassed.

Jesus knew both. He had been with the Father when man was created; he had seen sin's first tragic entrance into human experience; he had known from the eternities that he was to be the actual, effective sacrifice for sin's atonement and the sinner's redemption from its curse. When he painted this picture, he knew the love of his own heart that made him willing to come and to die on the cross that waited for him.

He also knew the longing in the heart of his Father. He understood God's amazing forbearance. In this picture we find that God, with an indescribable longing and yearning, waits for the sinner to "come to himself" because only then will he become conscious of his need and guilt and be moved to abhor and confess his sin. Here Jesus is saying to us that God feels toward every sinner as the father felt toward this son in the parable.

In the other two parables in this chapter the shepherd is seeking the lost sheep and the woman searching for the lost coin. In each instance there was unusual joy when that which was lost became found. Each parable closes with the refrain: "Even so, I tell you, there is joy before the angels of God over one sinner who repents" (Luke 15: 10, RSV) . The climax of that joy begins when the son has returned to the point where the father can see him coming down the road. What an unexpected welcome he received! So it has been with everyone who has traveled the same road in the same way.

12

The Greatness
and Graciousness of God

> *But while he was yet at a distance, his father saw him and had compassion, and ran and embraced him and kissed him. And the son said to him, "Father, I have sinned against heaven and before you; I am no longer worthy to be called your son." But the father said to his servants, "Bring quickly the best robe, and put it on him; and put a ring on his hand, and shoes on his feet; and bring the fatted calf and kill it, and let us eat and make merry; for this my son was dead, and is alive again; he was lost, and is found." And they began to make merry.*
>
> LUKE 15:20–24, RSV

A PHRASE FROM ALEXANDER MACLAREN captures the theme of the parable's last verses. It is, "When God forgives, he gives."

This parable was Jesus' way of telling us that the best gifts of God await those who so sincerely repent that they are ready to confess and pray for grace. Once the prodigal had committed himself to facing his father in this way, he discovered that his father's greatness and graciousness was beyond anything he ever hoped or dreamed. What happened to the penitent in the story has been confirmed in the experience of all who have met God as he did.

Most people think they have done quite enough and proved themselves to be big Christians when they forgive those who have wronged them. Not very many have run to meet the one who had sinned against them and greeted him with a hearty kiss of welcome. Too many of us have seemed to relish the discomfort of the confessor who acknowledges his wrong. It seems to be rather human to be puffed up with a glow of self-righteousness as another confesses his fault toward us. Certainly it is only a few who show the joyous graciousness of our God and Father, whom Jesus describes.

Penalties are the fruit of sin. They are the consequence of transgression. They are the outcome of yielding to temptation. In them the sinner is collecting the wages he has earned in the service of Satan.

All sin is, ultimately, against God. Everything that is sinful is contrary to God. Immediately, sin may be against oneself or against some other person. But finally it is against God, to whom all of us are responsible and to whom each of us must give an account.

All the while, however, it should be remembered that the sinner must face an unending series of inescapable consequences that are the inherent results of sin. God did not create them. Never has he enacted a lot of statutory legislation to which he has affixed various penalties that he imposes in punishment on sinners for their sins. The devil is the paymaster. Too many people get mixed up at this point. They forget that hell is something they create for themselves. Hell is a reality. Multiplied millions of people live in it in this world. It projects itself into the conscious life that survives death and continues through eternity for all who will not repent. But it is not God who sends people to hell; it is the sinners themselves. They have personally chosen the evil thing whose consequence is hell.

The father stopped the plea of the prodigal before he had finished making it. The younger son's free and open repentance brought the father's immediate forgiveness. There had never been a moment but that the father had been ready to forgive his son. The father never cherished any retaliatory vindictive desire to punish him for his sin. The only thing the father wanted was for the son to "come to himself." Until he did come to himself, his father could not forgive him. The sin within him made him spurn forgiveness, even as sin in the Pharisees and scribes made them scorn Jesus.

Here Jesus is bringing into sharp focus his Father God's attitude toward sinners. Primarily, God is grieved because of the hurt sinners suffer. Also, it is he who has lost their fellowship because they went away of their own choice and would not return. Men possess the power of choice and are clothed with the exclusive right to use it, but they are bound by the inescapable consequences.

No soul goes away from God to the far country with God's approval. God cannot go to the far country with a sinner, for to do so would be sin, and God would become the servant of Satan.

Many of the world's parents have known the grief that Jesus described. Their children left home and would not come back. They wanted to be away from home. They chose to break all communication with home. In their self-esteem and wrong thinking they positively committed themselves to the separation. All of us, in some measure or degree, have done this to God. There had never been a moment since the younger son had left home but that the father wanted him to return.

Had there ever been a day that he had not looked longingly down the road with yearning that he might discover the absent wanderer returning home? With patient forbearance he had kept unceasing vigil through all the years of the son's absence. He had never disowned him. He had never repudiated him. It is as though Jesus were saying to those who heard him there, and wherever the gospel is preached:

> For God so loved the world that he gave his only Son, that whoever believes in him should not perish but have eternal life. For God sent the Son into the world, not to condemn the world, but that the world might be saved through him. He who believes in him is not condemned; he who does not believe is condemned already, because he has not believed in the name of the only Son of God. And this is the judgment, that the light has come into the world, and men loved darkness rather than light, because their deeds were evil. For every one who does evil hates the light, and does not come to the light, lest his deeds should be exposed. But he who does what is true comes to the light, that it may be clearly seen that his deeds have been wrought in God. . . . He who believes in the Son has eternal life; he who does not obey the Son shall not see life, but the wrath of God rests upon him (John 3:16–21,36, RSV).

In this quotation Jesus gave his commentary on the spontaneous outreach of the hand of God for the hand of the returning sinner. The wrath of God mentioned in the last clause applies to Satan and the sinners who have made final, irrevocable partnership with Satan and who thereby are eternally committed to enmity against God and his son, Jesus Christ. They—Satan and impenitent sinners—by their unrelenting attack upon the sons and daughters of the living God evoke God's wrath in defensive resistance, that he may finally separate forever those who have returned to him from the attack of the hosts of iniquity.

God's pardon is a spontaneous outflow of love that eagerly celebrates the return of every sinner who has a contrite heart. The self-righteous elder brother looked upon it as a special favor heaped upon one who deserved to be damned. Thereby, he and his kind show how completely they misjudge God. Even the best of us have problems at this point. Mature saints, after the discipline of long years in the Father's fellowship, have a much greater understanding of the greatness and graciousness of God than has one who has not long been a Christian. But all of us suffer limitation because we cannot grasp the marvelous richness in its qualities and the vastness of the dimensions of God's love. One of the things that creates in the elder saints a more eager anticipation of heaven is the confident belief that there they will better understand God.

It is well for us to remember that God has always known all about us. His soul yearns for every person to have that kind of awakening, confession, and decision that sent the prodigal home. He has provided the way and opened the door for everyone to have it. His gospel is addressed always to whoever will believe on Jesus as Saviour with a heart-surrendering acceptance. He knows those who will accept Christ and those who will positively reject him. Knowing this, he is preparing for the return of each soul who will make the pilgrimage from the far country to the Father's house.

In this story there is a father who is waiting for the coming of a son whom he expected to return. So it will be with all the others. They will have made the journey away from God. They will have discovered themselves and their need and with contrite hearts made their journey to God in Christ.

The Father is waiting with the same welcome, the same rewards, and the same feast.

What are the gifts that God gives when he forgives?

He makes plain his forgiveness by direct action. He does
not hesitate. His running to meet the returning sinner is
proof of his eagerness. He proves it by treating them as
though they had never sinned. This is clearly set forth in the
parable. The father did not make any charges. He asked no
questions. He "ran and embraced him and kissed him." The
kiss was the signal and the seal of his forgiveness. It declared
that all was pardoned, for he knew the thoughts that had occupied the returning son's heart, the realizations that had
overwhelmed him, the penitence that had filled him with
contrition, the decision that had commanded his return, and
the craving of his soul for his Father's mercy.

Those who know how to interpret Scripture properly are
quite aware that one does not press every point that might
seem to be suggested in a parable. Parables contain material
symbols and elements that are the drapery of the story. These
are here in rich abundance as Jesus described the response
of the father to the son's return. Of one thing we can be very
certain: Jesus meant to communicate the idea of the richness
of the rewards with which the father commemorated the lost
son's return. He would have us to believe that those whom
God receives in the blessed relationship of sons are not to be
ranked socially in the fellowship of the kingdom of God as
hired servants. They are indeed servants. But they are sons
and daughters who delight to serve their Father. His desire
in their thought is the positive command for their obedience.

In the description Jesus gives us he makes it plain that his
Father cleanses, clothes, shoes, satisfies, and enjoys those
who respond to the invitation of his gospel.

This is not mentioned in the story. We are not presumptuous, however, in declaring that this son was ragged, dirty, and disheveled when his father ran to meet him and kissed him. Without question, the second gift that followed the return was cleansing. The long-lost son needed a bath. Regardless of one's theology, if he has ever experienced that great consciousness of personal sin which makes men travel the pilgrimage of repentance to confess to his Heavenly Father, he realizes in his own soul the truth of the lines:

> There is a fountain filled with blood
> Drawn from Immanuel's veins;
> And sinners, plunged beneath that flood,
> Lose all their guilty stains.
>
> WILLIAM COWPER

God would have his children be clean. He provides amply the gift and service for their cleansing.

The third gift of the father's bounty attests his heart's desire for his sons and daughters. "Bring quickly the best robe, and put it on him." Now that the stain and smell of the pigsty is washed away and is cast into the oblivion of everlasting forgetfulness, his servant is commanded to go to the wardrobe already prepared and bring forth its best robe, the righteousness of his God and Father, and put it on the returned son. He must be dressed, as all will be clad, with the best that God can provide for those who forsake the land of disobedience for the privileges of the Father's house.

What does this robe mean? The Scriptures have a lot to say on the subject. It is a familiar figure of speech that signifies qualities of character, elements of mind, and traits of heart. We are acquainted with the figures "arrayed in purity," "clothed with humility," "clad in zeal," and "vested with power." We read in Zechariah, " 'Remove the filthy garments from him.' And to him he said, 'Behold, I have taken your iniquity away from you, and I will clothe you with rich apparel' " (Zech. 3:4, RSV) . Then followed the commission from God to a great adventure in the divine service. Certainly we recall our Lord's parable of the man with the wedding garment and the apostle Paul's frequent use of "putting off the old man" and "putting on the new man." Who can forget the glorious spectacle of John's vision when he was on the Isle of Patmos, "He is clad in a robe dipped in blood, and the name by which he is called is The Word of God. And the armies of heaven, arrayed in fine linen, white and pure, followed him on white horses. . . . On his robe and on his thigh he has a name inscribed, King of kings and Lord of lords" (Rev. 19:13–14,16, RSV) .

These allusions, plus others which might be cited, indicate that this figure of the best robe that Jesus used here is a significant detail. In it he is presenting us the great thought that God's divine forgiveness to the confessing, contrite sinner is followed by his being clothed with a character that qualifies him to share at his Father's table. Can it be doubted that God's forgiveness transforms the lives of those who sincerely commit themselves to him in obedient surrender? Those who have traveled for years in the Christian pilgrimage know this transformation in their own lives. They can see its radiance in the lives of others. God's forgiveness and blessing cancels all the consequences of this sin of the contrite confessor, as far as God is concerned. Paul and other saints were aware that sin does leave scars, even after the healing touch of God. But God knows how to manage that and does it in his own way according to love, equity, and justice.

The thing that is being said here is that in Christ men become new creatures. God's forgiveness is real and is transforming. It recreates in the sinner the precious image and likeness of God. Thereto are added qualities that bespeak the sinner's having become a son of God after the similitude of Jesus Christ.

Free forgiveness from God furnishes the one forgiven motivation to press on to overcome evil, to loathe the sins that have been forgiven, and to resist with determination the lures of temptation. The experience of millions of pardoned souls testifies that they were clothed by God with new natures. This is the continuing urge that God plants in every soul who returns to him.

By the mercy of God many of us have not reached the depths of social degradation that befell this younger son. But each of us has turned his back on God. Not all of us have fallen into what the world calls gross sins, but we have all preferred our own way and positively avoided coming face to face with our God. The characters that we have made for ourselves, while under the dominion of self-will, have stuck to us like the poisonous shirt of Hercules. There are many who try to reform themselves, but in vain. They seek salvation by self-purification. Sooner or later all men become disillusioned about their ability to cleanse themselves from the corruptions of iniquity. Only Jesus Christ can provide the cleansing we need. It is he to whom the Father has delegated the ministry of our cleansing and clothing. Only he can satisfy the yearning of our souls to be right with God, our neighbors, and ourselves. Until he has met that need, our hearts will never be satisfied with anything that we can do for ourselves. And when he has supplied our need, our soul's first desire will be to be like him. Through him the grace of God clothes us with the robe of the righteousness of Jesus Christ. What a blessed gift this is that God gives to those whom he forgives!

The ring is the next gift that follows God's forgiveness. It is the symbol of the son's full restoration to the relationship which he had forfeited with his father. It is the declaration that he has grown up to the maturity of a trustworthy spiritual manhood and is now qualified to accept and use well the large responsibilities that his father would confer upon him. He was not capable of receiving nor qualified to use these things before he discovered his father's character and compassion.

The ring testified that the gulf that had separated them had been bridged. The repentance of the son enabled the father to pardon as well as forgive. No more is there an issue between them nor a conflict to be resolved. The son has repented of that which had separated them. His repentance and confession have closed the breach.

Years ago I read this story, where I do not recall. In a home there were the father and mother and two boys, the older eleven, the younger nine. The older had always been frail, had suffered much sickness, had grown slowly, and was light and undersized. The younger had always been vigorously healthy, had grown rapidly, weighed a few pounds more than his brother, and physically was much stronger. They had a wonderful mother whom each adored.

There came a rainy day when there was no school. It was too wet to go outside. There is a special devil that gets into boys with nothing to do when they have to stay indoors on a rainy day. These brothers were busy in their room, each with something of his own. Neither was disturbing the other. Finally, the younger lost interest in what he was doing and sat still a few moments. During this moment he unconsciously became envious of the pleasure his brother was having from what he was doing. Without their knowledge, the mother started to enter the room and saw what happened. The younger stood up and with a grim countenance swaggered over to his brother. With not a word he snatched away from him the book in which he was sketching and tore out a handful of its pages. When the older boy cried in protest, the younger snatched him out of the chair in which he was sitting.

Then the younger looked up and saw his mother. He was appalled by the look on her face and the sudden realization of the evil he had done. Ordinarily he was a child of good impulses—easy to get along with. When he saw his mother, his countenance fell. She was a wise mother. She knew the boy. Without a word she sadly walked away and went into the kitchen.

A few moments later the offending brother forced himself to go into the kitchen and asked, "Mother, isn't there something I can do to help you?"

The mother answered in tones that communicated the hurt of her heart: "There isn't anything that you can do for Mother now." He slunk away. His sin had separated him from his mother and brother. He had disrupted their fellowship. Sin had sent him into the far country of woe and left her at home with a saddened heart.

After a while he came back again and renewed his plea, "Mother, can't I put on my raincoat and go to the store and get something for you?"

To this request she answered again, "There isn't anything you can do for Mother now." The second time he went away. He had not repented. He had not recognized and confessed his sin. He was looking for an easy way out. He wanted to buy forgiveness with the little good work of running a convenient errand for his mother. In miniature he was trying to do what multiplied millions have undertaken and have always failed.

Another time he went back to his mother and tried to persuade her to let him help her in some way. She gave him the same answer. More time passed. Then he ran to his mother, threw his arms about her, and cried, "Oh, Mother, Mother, and Brother! Please forgive me. I did wrong. Won't you both please forgive me!" Like the father in the story, she threw her arms about his neck, mixed her tears with his, and kissed his away. The broken relationship was restored. His sin was pardoned. The separating chasm was bridged. They were united again. The issue was closed. It always is when love and honest contrition meet.

Repentance always brings forgiveness from the love that has been betrayed. Forgiveness brings pardon. Fellowship that has been broken is restored. Confidence and trust are regained. It means that life has begun all over again as if sin had never disrupted it.

David described it for all of us:

> Blessed is he whose transgression is forgiven,
>   whose sin is covered.
>
> . . . .
>
> I said, "I will confess my transgressions to the Lord";
>   then thou didst forgive the guilt of my sin.
> PSALM 32:1,5, RSV

The ring is a symbol that the wearer possesses the authority and resources of his master. Pharaoh plucked off his signet ring and placed it on the hand of Joseph. In the days of Jesus the honored steward who had in his charge the resources and business of his rich employer often was given the employer's signet ring, which testified that the steward had received all the authority of the owner for the management of what had been committed to his trust.

Without doubt, Jesus meant to tell us here what he spelled out more fully in other places. It is that sinners who return to God as this son did to his father become active partners with God. He gives them responsibility in the vast enterprises of his kingdom.

The shoes which the father ordered for his son are also meaningful. The feet were doubtless sorely bruised from the long journey. Sin had made him physically as well as spiritually shoeless. Shoes are a source of protection to the feet. They are essential to better service, for the possessor of shoes is prepared to render services that one who is barefoot cannot give. God's sons are to be shod for their journeys in the service of their Saviour. He has many missions for them that will take them far. Some of the traveling will be over roads that will be hard on their feet. There will be situations when their proper dignity demands shoes. These shoes the Father gives. They are the symbol of equipment for service. Paul said, "And having shod your feet with the equipment of the gospel of peace." In this special gift which God cannot give until he forgives, he provides for the needs his sons will find in their Father's service.

The son's prayer in the far country, "Father, make me," had been heard by his father while he was at home. The answer waited until his return. The answer was and is that God can trust and does trust the obedient heart. He makes available all his resources to supply the need of those who qualify by such a confession and plea.

These shoes affirm that their wearers, as the sons of God, serve as soldiers in his service, minister to the unmet needs of sinners and saints throughout the ages and in all the continents. Sometimes the wearer must carry his cross up various hills to his own Calvary, and in this world he must bear many afflictions. Those who faithfully bear responsibility are sustained by their Father God in all the trials, storms, persecutions, frustrations, pains, and burdens that life may bring. From his love nothing can separate them.

The first gift the prodigal sought was the last that he received. It was the tormenting pain of hunger that brought him to his senses. Perhaps most of us have missed a minor note that is clearly heard, even in his prayer, "Father, make me." Unconsciously the old habit of telling his father what he wanted still affected the patterns of his desire and speech. Even God's best saints find themselves entangled again and again at this point. Sometimes involuntarily, without being in the least aware, we keep on trying to tell God what to do for us and how and when to do it. The first half of his prayer, "Father, make me," brought forgiveness and opened all the storehouse of God to the prodigal. The last half, "as one of thy hired servants," the father ignored. God is competent to choose better for us than we are able to choose for ourselves.

When the son got home, he had to learn that he could not get bread on the terms that he desired. It surprised him to find that what he most wanted was not what he first needed. Once he had been bathed in the outflow of his father's love, clothed with the proper garments, invested with the ring, and shod with shoes becoming his father's son, he could not fail to be fed. Does not this say to us that after forgiveness every hunger of the heart will be met, needed nourishment will be provided, and "the meek shall eat and be satisfied"?

After these essential preparations, the parable comes to its final climax with the marvelous truth that in the banquet halls of heaven there is a gladsome feast to commemorate the new birth of every penitent sinner who by faith is reborn to become the son of the living God. Joyously the father orders, " 'Bring the fatted calf and kill it, and let us eat and make merry; for this my son was dead, and is alive again; he was lost, and is found.' And they began to make merry" (Luke 15:23–24, RSV).

Jesus is declaring that heaven celebrates the new birth of every sinner who returns to God. He shows that the way to lay hold on the greatness of God and to enter into the amazing riches of his graciousness is to travel the road with a contrite heart from the far country of self-will to the blessed city of "God's will be done."